England
A CONCISE HISTORY

England

A CONCISE HISTORY

F.E. HALLIDAY

With 230 illustrations

THAMES AND HUDSON

© 1964, 1980, 1989 and 1995
Thames and Hudson Ltd, London

First published in paperback in the United States
of America in 1980 by Thames and Hudson Inc.,
500 Fifth Avenue, New York, New York 10110

Revised edition 1989
Reprinted and updated 1995
Reprinted 1999

Library of Congress Catalog Card Number 79-67661
ISBN 0-500-27182-8

Printed and bound in Singapore

Contents

For
DONNET and MARTIN
though not just yet

Preface

I have written this book for a number of reasons. An aerial survey is the proper approach to any subject, for it is the whole that gives significance to the parts and inspires interest in detail. At school most of us learn something about a few 'periods', the sixteenth and eighteenth centuries perhaps, but little of what happened before and after, and there must be many who would welcome a History of England short enough to be grasped – and seen – as a whole.

One of the vexations of mortality is that we shall never know what happened next, but we can at least know what has happened, and have some idea, therefore, of what might happen. It is vitally important that we should know, for unless we do we are in an undiscovered country without a map. It is a disquieting thought that there are still so many people, indirectly responsible for directing the course of history, with little or no knowledge of where they have come from, where they are, or where they are going.

One thing that we should have learned by now, though we have not, is an understanding of nationalism. As an adolescent boy or girl demands independence, freedom from parental control, so does a people of the same race and speech demand freedom, unity and self-government. Both are equally natural processes and must be treated sympathetically, or frustration will lead only to a violent eruption of obstructed energy. If the legitimate demands of the American colonies and Ireland had been met, war and revolution would have been avoided, and they might now be members of the British Commonwealth. Unfortunately, again as with individual men, the unexpended energy of this first stage of nationalism is often directed against others, and self-realization becomes self-assertion and aggression: the England of the Hundred Years' War, the France of Louis XIV, the

Germany of William II. Again, there is a form of regressive nationalism, when a proud and powerful nation suffers defeat and humiliation, and attempts to recover its former glory. This it may do by a process of sublimation, achieving a moral or cultural ascendancy instead of a crude physical one, but a humiliated nation, like Hitler's Germany, is a potential source of danger. If we consider the world today it is not difficult to find examples of all three forms of nationalism – adolescent, aggressive, regressive – and it is this explosive force that a reading of history helps us to understand and, therefore, to control.

'History', wrote Gibbon, 'is little more than the register of the crimes, follies and misfortunes of mankind.' Yet, though Gibbon could not know, it is so very much more: the recorded fragment of man's evolutionary process, so pitifully near its beginning, the brief register of his constant struggle to create order out of chaos. For man is essentially creative, or he would not be here, and his destructive follies are merely aberrations in the grand design of his evolution. His highest activities, religion, art, and his quest for knowledge, are all a creation of order, and so is his struggle for a political organization in which he can live in freedom and peace. But order and freedom are not easily reconciled: the tyrant's freedom is the subjection of many, the freedom of many may mean license. The problem is the reconciliation of order with an extended freedom, and the final struggle is for an order in which all men can live in freedom and peace. By giving a proper emphasis to man's creative achievements and potentialities, history can help to hasten the process. Never has the task been more urgent than it is today, when a lapse into destructive folly might mean the return of history to its beginnings.

St Ives, Cornwall, 1963   F.E.H.

Publisher's Note

In this edition (1989), the opportunity has been taken to take the account to the end of the 1980s, and to update the 'Suggestions for Further Reading'. In the 1995 printing, further amendments relating to the 1990s have been made.

The sheer chalk cliffs of Kent and Sussex – unmistakably English (*opposite*).

And who in time knowes whither we may vent
The treasure of our tongue, to what strange shores
This gaine of our best glorie shal be sent,
T'inrich vnknowing Nations with our stores?
What worlds in th' yet vnformed Occident
May come refin'd with th' accents that are ours?

SAMUEL DANIEL, Musophilus, 1599

Book One

If we look at a geological and physical map of the British Isles, we see that the oldest rocks make the hills and mountains of the west and north, and that the newest form the comparatively flat country that lies south and east of a line running from Devonshire to north Yorkshire. This has been of supreme importance in British history, for the low land facing the Continent has always invited invasion. Yet this lower ground has its uplands: the limestone ridge that runs from Portland Bill and the Cotswolds to the Cleveland Hills, and the chalk hills of the Chilterns and Sussex and Dorset downs that radiate from the central boss of Salisbury Plain. As these limestone and chalk hills are well drained, they offered a refuge for primitive man above the marshy river valleys, and on Salisbury Plain is his greatest memorial, Stonehenge.

It is well to begin the history of England with Stonehenge, for it gives us a comprehensible time-scale, its main period of construction having been about as many years before the time of Christ as we live afterwards.

England had long been thinly peopled by Stone Age hunters and food-gatherers when, before 4000 BC, immigrants from the Continent arrived, settling partly on the chalk hills where they buried their dead in long barrows. They were the first farmers. A few centuries later their descendants, perhaps with new immigrant groups, began the custom of building great stone tombs, commonest along the coast from Cornwall to the Orkneys. By 2500 BC the first phase at Stonehenge had been completed: the outer bank and ditch, apparently a sanctuary connected with a sun cult.

17

The dawn of English history – Stonehenge.

Stonehenge from the air, showing the circular earthwork, outer circle of stones, and inner horseshoe of trilithons.

About 2000 BC these neolithic people may have been joined by others from Holland and the Rhineland, the Beaker Folk, so called from their characteristic drinking-vessel. They brought a knowledge of metal-working and from Pembrokeshire transported some eighty great bluestones which they erected in a double circle at the centre of the Stonehenge sanctuary. Trade and metal tools brought prosperity, gradually immigrants and natives became one people, and their memorial is the huge stone circle and central horseshoe of trilithons, the ruins of which we see today.

The builders of Stonehenge were already a mixed people, and this mixture was to be enriched by successive invaders of the country for another two thousand years and more. As the complex geology of Britain makes its scenery more varied than that of any other small country, so the fusion of peoples, from south, east and north, has produced a variety, richness and vigour that must partly account for their astonishing expansion after medieval times. Perhaps it also accounts for their greatest glory, their literature, for no language is so rich in words as English, in

Bronze Age beaker.

Trethevy Quoit, Cornwall. A Late Stone Age burial chamber, originally covered with a mound of earth. The name derives from the legends about Cornish giants who were said to play quoits with the capstones.

which *freedom* is also *liberty* and *independence*, and *red* is *scarlet*, *vermilion*, *crimson*, *cardinal* and *gules*.

There were other minor invasions before the coming of the Celts, who from about 800 BC moved west from their Central European homeland. They were a tall, fair-skinned and blue-eyed people, farmers skilled in the working of bronze, and later of iron. In the second century BC gradual infiltration into Britain became invasion by warrior bands armed with weapons of iron. These Celts conquered Kent and much of southern England, pressed into Cornwall in search of tin, spread north and in many parts established themselves as an aristocratic élite. Hilltop fortresses, first developed in the Late Bronze Age, became imposing strongholds, like Maiden Castle in Dorset, as native Britons fought invading Celts for control of the countryside. The conquerors imposed their language on the natives, its Gaelic form in Ireland and Scotland, the Brythonic in England and Wales; and it was the Brythonic tribe that gave its name to the whole

The multiple ramparts of Maiden Castle.

country, though the most powerful was that of the Belgae in the south-east.

It was an Age of Iron, though not altogether barbaric. The Celts imported the luxuries of the Mediterranean, their priests, the Druids, were the teachers and administrators of the age, and their craftsmen developed an abstract, curvilinear art that is one of the glories of western civilization.

These then were the Britons, now predominantly Celtic, who in their war chariots opposed the landing of Julius Caesar and his legions in 55 and 54 BC. But Caesar's summer expeditions were a failure, and it was almost another hundred years before the Romans came again.

Bronze Celtic shield, studded with red enamel.

Bronze mirror, showing the Celtic design on the back. The front was polished bronze.

During the century between Caesar's expeditions and the second coming of the legions, there was a peaceful Roman penetration of Britain. Under the Belgic chief Cunobelin, Shakespeare's Cymbeline, much of southern England was for the first time united under a single ruler, *Rex Brittonum* as he was called. Roman merchants settled here, slaves, iron and corn were exported in exchange for eastern luxuries, and in Colchester, his capital, Cymbeline struck coins after the Roman pattern. When he died, however, his kingdom collapsed, and in AD 43 the Roman emperor Claudius sent an army to add Britain to his empire.

In spite of the fierce resistance of the wild tribes of the north, and of Queen Boadicea in Norfolk, the Roman legions soon occupied England. Wales, too, was eventually subdued, but the Roman occupation of the islands was virtually confined to England: there was no attempt to invade Ireland, Wales was too mountainous for civilian settlement, Scotland too wild and warlike, and Cornwall too barren and remote. In the west and north, therefore, the old Celtic tribalism remained, and the Romans sealed off these dangerous areas by building forts at Caerleon, Chester and York, each the headquarters of a legion, and a great defensive wall across the north of England, from Solway to the mouth of Tyne.

London, on the site where the Thames could most easily be bridged, was also walled, and from this inland port radiated the straight paved roads that led to the garrison towns: Ermine Street and Watling Street, as the Saxons were to call them, the one to Lincoln, York and the Wall, the other to Chester, and a third to Silchester, Cirencester, Gloucester and Caerleon. A fourth road, the Fosse Way, ran from Lincoln to Cirencester and Exeter, the last outpost in the south-west. London is a Celtic name, as are the names of most of our rivers, but many of the towns that the Romans built along their roads, from Lancaster to Winchester and Chichester, still have the Latin termination *castra*, a camp or fortified town.

The Roman occupation was a paternal one, bringing prosperity and orderly government to a disorderly, and therefore dangerous, province on the frontier of empire. Some towns were allowed self-

Coin of Cymbeline,
'King of the Britons'.

government, and the Britons became citizens of the Roman Empire. Few of the occupying soldiers, civil servants and merchants would come from Rome or Italy, and probably the majority were romanized Gauls from France, Celts and kinsmen of the British. Intermarriage, therefore, would not greatly affect the native stock, though the native tongue absorbed many Latin words.

For some three centuries under the Pax Romana the Britons of the southern half of England knew little or nothing of war. Towns were centres of civilization, and Bath and Verulamium emulated the elegance of Rome; the ports shipped lead from Shropshire and the Mendips, iron from the Weald and Forest of Dean, even gold from Wales, and corn was exported to feed the populace of the imperial capital.

Hadrian's Wall – the northern limit of Roman occupation.

The Roman baths
at Aquae Sulis (Bath).

There was more of the old Celtic way of life in the country, but the wealthier British farmers, their land cultivated by serfs or slaves, lived in villas adorned with frescoes and mosaics and warmed by central heating. For them and the prosperous town-dwellers, educated in the art and literature of Rome, the second century was perhaps the most idyllic in our history.

By this time there were a few Christians in eastern England, and at the beginning of the fourth century the province produced its first martyr, St Alban. The Empire was still pagan, and the religion of the Britons a confusion of Roman and Celtic cults, but soon after the martyrdom of Alban the Emperor Constantine made Christianity the imperial religion, and a British Church was soon a flourishing institu-

Roman mosaic pavement, with head of a sea god. Verulamium.

Roman under-floor heating. Hypocaust at Chedworth Roman Villa in the Cotswolds.

tion. It had not time, however, to convert more than a fraction of the population, for the Empire, rotten at the centre, was beginning to break up. Barbarians were battering at its frontiers, and in 367 the wild Celts of the north, the Picts and Scots, overran the Wall, while Saxon pirates landed in the east, and ravaged the greater part of England.

For another fifty years the Romans managed to hold the province, but the end was in sight. They could not afford to keep an army of forty thousand men along the Welsh and Scottish marches and along the 'Saxon Shore' from Norfolk to Kent, and at the beginning of the fifth century they withdrew. They had been here for four hundred years, and now the civilized and unwarlike Britons were left to the mercy of the barbarians who surrounded them.

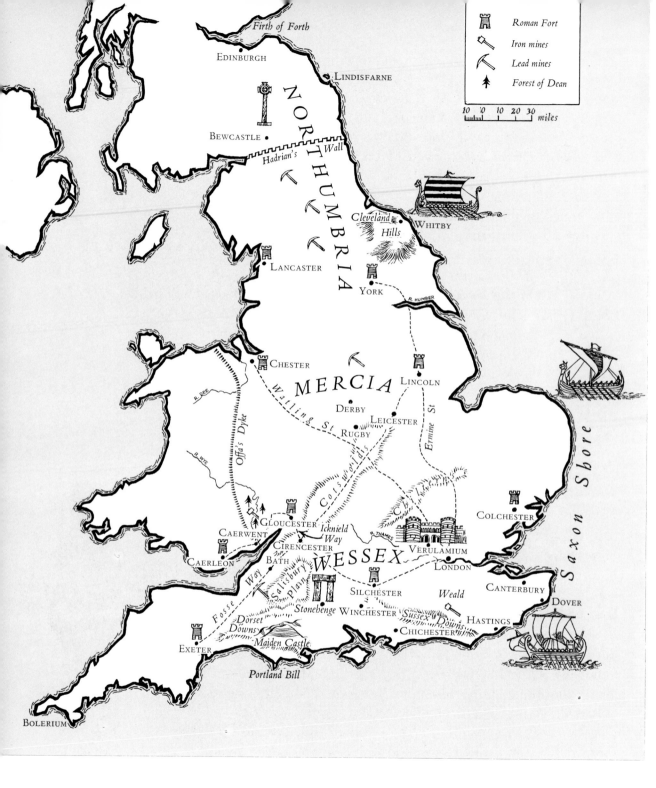

10 10 10 20 30 *miles*

Firth of Forth

EDINBURGH

LINDISFARNE

N O R T H U M B R I A

BEWCASTLE

Hadrian's Wall

Cleveland Hills

WHITBY

LANCASTER

YORK

R. HUMBER

CHESTER

M E R C I A

LINCOLN

R. DEE

Offa's Dyke

Watling St.

DERBY

LEICESTER

Ermine St.

R. WYE

RUGBY

Cotswolds

Chilterns

COLCHESTER

GLOUCESTER

Icknield Way

CAERWENT

CIRENCESTER

R. THAMES

VERULAMIUM

CAERLEON

BATH

W E S S E X

LONDON

Fosse Way

Salisbury Plain

SILCHESTER

Weald

CANTERBURY

DOVER

Stonehenge

WINCHESTER

Sussex Downs

HASTINGS

Dorset Downs

CHICHESTER

EXETER

Maiden Castle

Portland Bill

BOLERIUM

S a x o n   S h o r e

Prehistoric, Roman and Anglo-Saxon England.

The Angles and Saxons were barbaric Teutonic tribes, tall and fair, who lived between the mouth of the Rhine and Denmark. They were primarily farmers, but the promise of plunder in the neighbouring island roused all their piratical instincts, and in the course of the fifth century they advanced from east to west of England, up the rivers in their ships, along the Roman roads, slaughtering and enslaving the Britons, sacking and burning towns and villas. Many of the Britons fled west, into Wales and Cornwall, taking with them their Roman culture, language and Christianity, and it was at the end of this century, about 500, that one of these romanized Celts, Ambrosius Aurelianus, checked the English at the battle of Badon, somewhere in Dorset or Wiltshire. This is the period of the half-legendary King Arthur, the British champion of Christianity against the heathen English.

It is also the period of St Patrick, son of a western British priest, who spent his life converting the Irish Celts to Christianity. So successful was his work that Ireland became a land of monasteries and missionaries, the most important of whom was St Columba, who in 563 founded a monastery on the little island of Iona, from which the Celts of Scotland were to be converted.

It was a strange reversal of the situation: instead of a civilized and Christian England surrounded and menaced by pagan Celts, a barbaric and pagan England threatened the more civilized and partly Christian Celts, the Welsh, or 'foreigners', as the English called them. There were four of these Celtic countries: Scotland, Wales, Cornwall – for the English had not yet overrun the Devonian peninsula – and Ireland. In this dark age Ireland was a centre of light, its monks and saints, when not fighting, jealously treasuring a knowledge of Latin literature and lovingly illuminating their manuscripts of the Gospels.

The civilization of the Celts, however, must not be over-estimated. They were a quarrelsome people, who found it difficult to unite into larger units than the clan or tribe; it is significant that their monasteries were congregations of hermits living in separate cells, and that for them the parish has always been more important than for the English. Moreover memories of Roman civilization were growing dim in Wales and Cornwall: Latin spelling, and even the letters falter on tombstones of

Cross of Patrick and Columba, Kells, Co. Meath.

Tintagel, the Cornish headland associated with King Arthur. The castle in the foreground is medieval, but on the top can be seen the site of a Celtic monastery of the Dark Ages.

Cornish Christians of Arthur's time, and before long the old Celtic way of life reasserted itself, and Rome was only a legend.

For the English the sixth century was one of consolidation and settlement, for they had destroyed almost every trace of the civilization of the Romans, save their roads and pheasants. There was fighting, of course, among the many petty kingdoms, among the North and South

Folk of Norfolk and Suffolk, the South and East Saxons of Sussex and Essex, but gradually three greater kingdoms began to emerge: Northumbria, north of the Humber, Mercia in the Midlands, and Wessex in the south.

Then at the end of the century Pope Gregory sent a monk, Augustine, to convert the English to Christianity. He landed in Kent in 597, converted its king, and became the first Archbishop of Canterbury, the Kentish capital. Northumbria, too, was converted, not altogether by Roman missionaries, however, but also by Celtic missionaries led by St Aidan, a monk from Iona who had founded a monastery on the island of Lindisfarne. By the middle of the seventh century all England was converted, though not to the same form of Christianity. Celtic Christianity had come to England three hundred years before that of St Augustine, and there were slight differences and inevitable jealousies. To decide which should be accepted a synod of bishops was called at Whitby in 664. The decision was in favour of the new Roman form.

It was of immense importance. It foreshadowed the future struggle with Rome and, more immediately, brought England again within the influence of the Mediterranean and into contact with the new civilization of Europe. Then, the Church through its bishops brought literacy and learning to kings and their councils, a greater humanity to their laws and conduct, and its organization into dioceses and parishes prefigured a corresponding political organization and unity.

30

Shaft of the Northumbrian cross at Bewcastle.

The time was not yet, however. The seventh century was that of the supremacy of Northumbria, whose great king Edwin advanced its frontier to the Forth, where he built his stronghold of Edinburgh. It was in this northern kingdom that English art and letters flowered for the first time: in the illuminated *Lindisfarne Gospels*, sculptured crosses like that at Bewcastle, the poems of Caedmon, and the Latin *Ecclesiastical History* of Bede, the story of the recent conversion and the first great prose work written by an Englishman.

St Matthew, from the Lindisfarne Gospels, *c.* 700.

Lindisfarne Abbey, Holy Island, headquarters of the Celtic missionaries who helped convert northern England to Christianity. The monastery was restored by the Normans.

Ninth-century
harvesters.

The eighth century saw the supremacy of Mercia, whose King Offa drove the Welsh behind the great dyke that he built along the border from the mouth of Wye to the Dee.

Then, at the beginning of the ninth century the king of Wessex, Egbert, subdued the Celts of Devon and Cornwall, defeated the Mercians in battle, and so became the first king of all England, at least in name.

For his dominion was shadowy. The English had been here for four hundred years, as long as the Romans, but they were still primitive farmers living in scattered villages and townships, their open ploughlands and meadows separated from those of their neighbours by forest and waste. There was no city life, for they shunned the haunted ruins of the Romans, though one Englishman at least was moved to pity by the sight of the ruins of Bath:

> Wrætlic is þaes wealstan wyrde gebræcon
> burgstede burston brosnað enta geweorc
> Hrofas sind gehrorene hreorge torras
> hrungeat-torras berofen hrim on lime
> scearde scurbeorge scorene gedrorene
> ældo under-eotone

'Wondrous is its wallstone: fates have broken, have shattered the city, the work of giants is decaying. The roofs are fallen, the towers in ruins, the towers with barred doors destroyed, frost on the mortar, the ramparts down, fallen, with age under-eaten.' It is only a fragment, a ruin like the city it laments, but it is the most personal and poignant of all Old English poems.

Without an organized central government and efficient army, the king was dependent on the loyalty of local landowners, the thegns, and of the ealdermen and bishops who composed his council, or Witan, and these farmers, rooted in the soil, no longer the fierce warriors who had conquered the Britons four centuries before, were ill-prepared to repel even more ferocious invaders than their ancestors had been. These were the Northmen, the Vikings of Norway and the Danes: tall, powerful, fair-haired pirates who in their long ships were to colonize Iceland and Greenland, and discover America. Adventurous and virile, these heathen giants soon settled into the lands they conquered, adding new vigour to the native stock, and were to inspire in the English their long-forgotten passion for the sea and an acceptance of the town life they had never known.

King Alfred's Jewel.

Figurehead
of a Viking ship.

Their raids had begun in the eighth century, but by the middle of the ninth had become invasion. From Norway the Vikings conquered northern Scotland and the Hebrides, the Isle of Man, Cumberland and Lancashire, and finally Ireland, where they brought to an end the golden age of Celtic civilization. Meanwhile the Danes overran eastern England, Yorkshire became a Danish kingdom, and even the south-west was threatened. In 871, however, they were checked at Ashdown in the Berkshire hills by the young king of Wessex, Alfred.

A few years later Alfred forced the Danes to come to terms: to accept Christianity and retire behind the line of Watling Street, into the Danelaw and its towns with characteristic Danish endings – Rugby, Derby – leaving him master of the south and west. There, based on Winchester, capital of Wessex, he organized its defence, creating an efficient army and building a fleet, so that later Danish invaders were diverted to northern France, where their settlement became known as Normandy, the province of the Northmen.

Rough Justice
a Saxon King and his Witan.

Alfred was then free to repair the ravages of the Danish incursions. He rebuilt churches, brought over foreign scholars, founded schools for the sons of his noblemen, began the compilation of the *English Chronicle*, and himself translated a number of books from the Latin, including Bede's *Historia Ecclesiastica*, and to his version of Gregory's *Cura Pastoralis* he added a preface describing the decay of learning:

Swa clæne hio wæs oðfeallenu on Angelkynne ðætte swiðe feawe wæron behionan Humbre þe hiora ðenunga cuðan understandan on Englisc, oððe furðum an ærendgewrit of Lædene on Englisc areccan.

'So clean was it fallen away in England that very few there were on this side of the Humber who could understand their service-books in English, or even translate a letter from Latin into English.' It was to be three hundred years before the language we know began to emerge.

Alfred died in 900, and thanks to his work the greater part of the tenth century was something of a golden age. The Danes to the east of Watling Street were subdued and absorbed, and the Welsh and even the Danes of Ireland did

Saxon tower of Earls Barton Church, Northants.

PORTA TVR:CORPVS:EADWARDI·REGIS:AD·ECCLE:
PETRI

Burial of Edward the Confessor in his Abbey of Westminster.

homage to the English kings. When, however, the great King Edgar died in 975, he was succeeded by the worthless Ethelred. The kingdom fell into confusion, the Danes renewed their attacks from Scandinavia, and in 1016 England submitted to a Danish king, Canute, becoming indeed part of a great Danish empire that included Norway as well as Denmark.

After the death of Canute's sons in 1042 the empire collapsed, and Ethelred's son, Edward the Confessor, was restored to the throne of an independent England. As Edward's mother was a Norman, he was brought up in Normandy during the twenty-six years of Danish rule, and not unnaturally returned more French than English, bringing with him Norman friends and clergy. For, monkish in his ideals, his chief interest was the Church, his main memorial the foundation of Westminster Abbey, to be near which he moved the royal residence from the walled city of London to his new Palace of Westminster. It was a momentous removal, for London, already much the biggest and

Duke William hears that Harold is advancing towards Hastings.

wealthiest of English towns, was to become the centre of resistance against royal tyranny.

While the pious Edward was thus employed, the real ruler of England was the leader of the anti-Norman party, Harold, Earl of Wessex. When, therefore, Edward died childless at the beginning of 1066, the Witan elected Harold as his successor.

Harold was Edward's brother-in-law, but Duke William of Normandy was Edward's cousin, with some claim, therefore, to the throne, and he prepared to seize what he professed to believe his rightful inheritance. Harold confidently awaited his coming, but at the last moment was called upon to repel a Norwegian invasion in Yorkshire, and while he was away William landed at Pevensey. Harold raced south to meet him, but before all the English forces had arrived William attacked, and by the evening of October 14th, on a low ridge north of Hastings, Harold and the flower of the English nobility lay dead.

The death of Harold at Hastings.

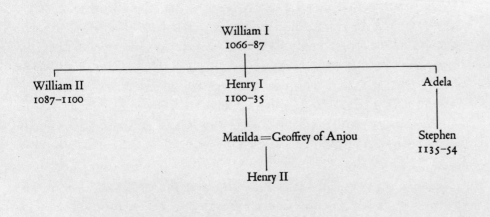

```
                        William I
                        1066-87
                           │
    ┌──────────────────────┼──────────────────────┐
William II              Henry I                  Adela
1087-1100              1100-35                      │
                          │                      Stephen
                 Matilda = Geoffrey of Anjou     1135-54
                          │
                       Henry II
```

Had England been a united country the battle of Hastings alone would not have decided its history; it would not have been conquered in a single fight by some twelve thousand men, however efficiently organized and armed. But England was united only in name, and there was no immediate resistance. London was overawed, and at Christmas William was crowned at Westminster. A few years later there were risings, but as they were uncoʼordinated they gave William the chance to crush them one by one; Yorkshire was laid waste, and after the surrender of Hereward the Wake in the Isle of Ely, England was completely subjugated.

The conquest had been relatively easy; the problem was to hold it. Although William combined a Viking vigour with a Latin genius for organization, and his duchy of Normandy was the most efficient state in Europe, without the means of exercising direct control from the centre, without trained civil servants and lawyers to administer all corners of the kingdom in his name, his only recourse was to delegate power to his earls and barons by the imposition of a systematic feudalism. The first step was to dispossess the English nobles who had survived Hastings and the rebellions and to distribute their estates among his followers.

The word *feudalism* is derived from *fee*, an estate in land, and the feudal system was based on the tenancy – not ownership – of land. The king was the owner, and from him his tenants-in-chief held their estates in return for military service with a prescribed number of knights, sub-tenants held from these great men, and at the bottom of the scale was the serf or villein who paid the rent for his few acres by working on his lord's estate. The English had had a form of feudalism, but it had never been rigidly enforced, and there had been thousands of small independent freeholders. Now, however, every man was to have his lord.

Moreover, every lord was to administer his own justice – or injustice – in his own private court: from that of the tenant-in-chief who dealt with disputes among his vassals, to the manorial court of the village. It is true that the king was represented in every shire by his officer, the sheriff, who presided over his public Shire Court, but the sheriffs were generally feudal earls and the judges merely the untrained leading freemen of the county, who administered traditional local law. For as yet there was no Common Law, no law common to the whole country, and of course there was no Parliament. If the king wanted advice he merely consulted the tenants-in-chief who composed his Great Council. Yet it was from this assembly that Parliament was to develop, as well as the Curia Regis, or King's Court, a select committee of the Council that soon came to have specialized financial and judicial functions.

Rank and power, then, depended on the holding of land, almost the only form of wealth, and the unit was the manor. The typical manor was a few great unenclosed fields and a cluster of hovels about the church. Here lived the peasants, the villeins, bound to the soil they tilled. There were normally three of these open fields in each of which the villein held some ten scattered strips of about an acre, in return for which he worked so many days a week on his lord's domain. He had his share in the common meadow and rights of pasture in the surrounding woods and waste, but he had to grind his corn in his lord's mill. If his lord held only one manor he would live there most of the year, but if he were a great man he would be seen only occasionally

Reapers, directed by the Reeve, a villein who acted as overseer for the lord of the manor.

when he and his servants arrived to eat its produce, for the manor was virtually self-supporting, transport of food was difficult, and men had to come to its source of supply.

Before the Conquest the lord of the manor was an Englishman, mixing freely with his tenants, but now he was a Norman living remotely in a wooden fort on top of a mound; a foreigner speaking unintelligible French, and the cows, pigs and sheep that the English villein bred and killed for him became the beef, pork and mutton of his table. It was a harsh and rigid system, for the villein was desperately poor, had few rights against his superiors, and was unable to leave the manor; yet he was secure in his tenure, and there was no unemployment.

Without the interpenetration of the country by royal officials, the smooth working of the feudal system depended on the king's ability to control his great vassals, and to strengthen his position William distributed their estates over various parts of the kingdom, so that there should be no great concentration of power. There were some necessary exceptions along the unsettled borders of Wales and Scotland, and it was these great Marcher Lords of the west and north who were the greatest danger to the royal authority. It was after the revolt of one of them, the Earl of Hereford, who called out his sub-tenants against him, that William exacted an oath making each tenant responsible directly to the king, instead of, as in France, to his immediate overlord, a severe restriction of the powers of his tenants-in-chief. William also separated church courts from secular courts so that the clergy should not come under feudal jurisdiction, a move of immense significance. Finally, he

41

Built to subdue the English: the Norman keep of Castle Rising, Norfolk.

Norman tympanum, Quenington church, Gloucestershire.

Domesday Book: so called because there was no appeal from its judgment.

West front of the Norman church at Iffley, near Oxford, the door rich in chevron and beak-head ornament.

The great Norman nave of Durham Cathedral.

ordered the compilation of the Domesday Book of 1086: a detailed survey of all the manors of England, showing who held them, their size, number of villeins, amount of stock and value. This showed at a glance the power of every tenant and, equally important, how much could be extracted from him in taxes.

It was an order certainly, far better than disorder, but an imposed order, a despotism, with liberty for the king, a limited liberty for his great subjects, and servitude for the great majority. The barons resented this limitation of their power, so much less than that enjoyed by the feudal nobility of France, and were ever watchful for the opportunity to assert what they considered to be their rights.

As the secular landowners were now nearly all Normans, so were the chief officers of the Church, the bishops and heads of monasteries. The English Archbishop of Canterbury was replaced by the Norman

A twelfth-century schoolroom, apparently a writing lesson.

Lanfranc, and under him the old English laxity was galvanized into Norman efficiency, and a great period of building began.

For the Normans were great builders, in the massive round-arched Romanesque style that was the legacy of imperial Rome. William I built the Tower of London, William II Westminster Hall, and some fifty more great castles, from Rochester to Launceston in Cornwall and Richmond in Yorkshire, were built to keep down the English. But citadels of another order were the parish churches, cathedrals and monasteries of the period. Even the most modest churches, like those of the Cotswolds, were enriched with carvings, and cathedral windows, as at Canterbury, filled with the splendid stained glass that is the unique contribution of the Middle Ages to the art of Europe; and the monasteries were the schools, universities and libraries that kept learning alive during this grim century.

The despotic Conqueror was followed by his sons, the rapacious Rufus, William II, and the severe but efficient Henry I, whose most characteristic addition to the administrative system was the Court of Exchequer, for the better collecting of taxes. It was a very important reform, however, for it was the beginning of the division of the Curia Regis into specialized departments staffed by trained men. The president of the new court was the Justiciar, who became the chief minister of the realm.

Henry gave England peace, and when he died in 1135 the vanquished English were disciplined and unified as never before. Indeed, it may be argued that the Norman Conquest was the best thing that could have happened to them. Without this discipline they might have stagnated in their island home, a number of semi-independent principalities eventually to be absorbed in Scandinavia. The Normans imposed unity and linked them permanently to the culture of southern Europe.

But the opportunity that the barons were awaiting had come. Henry left no legitimate son, there was a disputed succession and, as the country was still little more than a patchwork of feudal estates, order quickly crumbled into chaos. Some of the barons supported the Council's choice of Stephen, son of the Conqueror's daughter, others Henry I's daughter Matilda, and there followed almost twenty years of civil war. It was each baron for himself, and the last compiler of the *English Chronicle*, a monk of Ely, described the horrors to which his countrymen were subjected: 'They greatly oppressed the wretched people by making them work at their castles, and when the castles were finished they filled them with devils and evil men. Then they took those whom they thought to have any goods, both men and women, and put them in prison for their gold and silver, and tortured them with pains unspeakable.' It was a terrifying lapse into anarchy from the slow creation of order.

Stephen himself was an amiable man, but events were beyond his control, and it was fortunate for England that her next king was one of the greatest she has ever had.

Twelfth-century
stained glass in
Canterbury Cathedral.

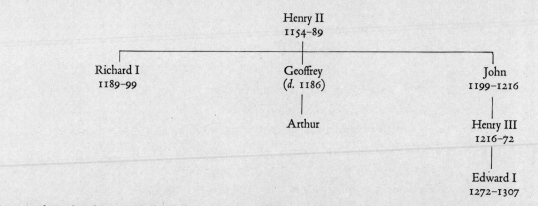

```
                          Henry II
                          1154-89
         ┌───────────────────┼───────────────────┐
    Richard I            Geoffrey                John
    1189-99              (d. 1186)              1199-1216
                            │                      │
                         Arthur                 Henry III
                                                1216-72
                                                   │
                                                Edward I
                                                1272-1307
```

Henry II, buried in his French dominions, at Fontevrault in Anjou.

5
*The Making
of the Nation
1154-1307*

Henry Plantagenet, first of the Angevin kings, inherited the vigour of his grandfather, the blood of English kings from his mother, Anjou from his father, Aquitaine from his wife, all western France, therefore, from Normandy to Gascony and the Pyrenees. Save Normandy, these French provinces of the Angevin Empire did not belong to the English crown; Henry held them merely as Count of Anjou and feudal vassal of the King of France, but they made him far more powerful than his suzerain and than the Norman kings who had preceded him. Although only twenty-one, he had governed his French possessions for some years, and now he turned to the restoration of order in England.

The first thing was to demolish the hundreds of unlicensed castles built in Stephen's reign. Then, instead of military service he demanded money from the barons, which enabled him to hire mercenaries responsible to himself alone. To keep order at home he raised a militia composed of all freemen, and prescribed how they were to be armed. It is worth pausing to consider the implications of this, and the change that had taken place in the last century. The Norman Conqueror had relied on his feudal nobility to keep down the English; Henry Plantagenet called in the English to help him control the nobility. They were willing enough; an efficient despotism was infinitely preferable to baronial anarchy.

Of more lasting importance were Henry's legal reforms. He transformed the Curia Regis into a regular court of trained officials and lawyers. He dismissed most of the feudal sheriffs and replaced them with these men. Others were made into a special court of justice, the King's Bench, and, most important of all, he sent out travelling judges, Justices in Eyre, who carried a 'common law' into every Shire Court of the country. This royal justice was popular because it was cheaper and less arbitrary than that of the feudal courts, and because the jury system began to replace the barbarous trial by combat. A national system of law and local government and a civil service were beginning to take shape.

All this meant a further reduction in the power of the barons, as revenue was diverted from their private courts to the royal exchequer. It also meant an immense increase of the king's power, for the government was now one of professionals, both at the centre and in the shires, and the sheriffs and travelling justices carried the royal authority and law into every part of the kingdom. It was an order no longer entirely dependent on the character of the king; it would survive a worthless or absentee monarch, and Henry himself spent half of his reign in France; an order that drew strength from the common people, now united by a common law and loyalty to the crown.

Henry even established some sort of order in Ireland, for the first time invaded from England, and was recognized, at least in name, as its king.

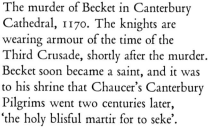

The murder of Becket in Canterbury Cathedral, 1170. The knights are wearing armour of the time of the Third Crusade, shortly after the murder. Becket soon became a saint, and it was to his shrine that Chaucer's Canterbury Pilgrims went two centuries later, 'the holy blisful martir for to seke'.

In one thing he failed. His Archbishop, Thomas Becket, opposed his attempt to bring clergy who had been convicted of crime in the church courts before the king's court for sentence. As a result Becket was murdered in his cathedral and became a martyr. Henry had to submit to the Pope, and throughout the Middle Ages the clergy – and anybody who could read Latin might claim to be a clerk – could commit the gravest crimes with no worse punishment than reduction to the level of laymen.

Apart from this failure Henry's reign was triumphantly successful, and the measure of his success is that the country did not revert to baronial anarchy under his two sons.

The first was the romantic sportsman Richard I, who spent all but a few months of his reign crusading against the Moslems in the Holy Land or fighting his suzerain in France, where he was killed in 1199.

Although Richard was an expensive monarch who cared nothing for England, he was a popular hero, but his brother John was perhaps the most detestable of all English kings. Misusing the enormous power bequeathed him by his father, he extorted money from his subjects, from the Church, Norman baron and English villein alike, to defend his French possessions, but incompetently lost all his northern provinces, including Normandy. He murdered his young nephew Arthur, who had a better claim to the throne. He quarrelled with the Pope over the appointment of Stephen Langton as Archbishop, and then abjectly surrendered, agreeing to pay tribute for England as the Pope's vassal. Langton became the leader of the barons who, tired of his incompetent tyranny, forced him to swear to observe the laws, but John broke his oath, plunged his country into civil war, and died, opportunely and characteristically, by overeating.

Yet the misgovernment of John was by no means altogether a misfortune. Had he been another Henry II England might have become an established despotism. As it was, his barons were driven into revolt and, supported by the Church and for the first time by the English people, in 1215 they forced him to sign Magna Carta.

It was a purely selfish class measure, setting forth the privileges of the aristocracy and Church, without mention of the great majority of Englishmen, the villeins. The barons could not destroy the administrative system of Henry II, but they might become even more powerful than they had been if they could control the government at the centre. Magna Carta checked the despotic power of the king, and was the first step in the century-long struggle to establish a baronial oligarchy. Clause 39, however, was to have a wider application than they anticipated: 'No freeman shall be arrested or imprisoned or dispossessed or outlawed or banished or in any way molested, nor will we go upon him

Charter of King John, 9 May 1215,
providing for the annual election
of a mayor of London.

nor send upon him, except by the lawful judgment of his peers and the law of the land.' There were, of course, few freemen apart from the nobility and knights, but their numbers would increase.

In fact the number of freemen was increasing fairly rapidly at this time. John, ever short of money, accelerated a process that had already begun of selling charters of self-government to towns that could afford to pay for this privilege, and in his reign London secured the right of electing its own mayor. It was much the biggest town, but others were growing, for so was trade, particularly the export of wool. Then, Oxford and Cambridge had become university towns and, though there were at first no colleges, the scholars, most of them poor, added greatly to the intellectual ferment of the thirteenth century.

For it was an exciting century of change. Shortly after Magna Carta the friars arrived in England. Unlike the monks, they did not stay in their monasteries, but went out to help and preach to the poor. They opened boarding houses for the students of Oxford, and here the most famous of the Franciscans, Roger Bacon, taught scientific methods of observation and experiment. He is the first clear light in the medieval darkness, the Newton of his age.

The beginning of constitutional government. Magna Carta, sealed by King John at Runnymede, June 1215.

The first university college – Merton, founded in Oxford in 1274.

Many of these university men learned to be lawyers in the specialized courts that were developing from the Curia Regis. They worked in Westminster Hall, but soon after the foundation of the first colleges at Oxford and Cambridge they built themselves lodgings, the Inns of Court, between Westminster and London, so linking the political and commercial capitals. The law was the main ladder by which the poor layman could climb into the ranks of the great.

Meanwhile the struggle between king and barons continued. John had left the country torn by civil war, and his son Henry III was only a boy of nine, but order was restored, and when Henry came of age he tried to return to the despotism of his grandfather. By now, particularly since the loss of Normandy, the barons were more English than French, and Henry infuriated them by filling offices with foreign favourites, as he infuriated the Church by selling benefices to foreigners, and the people as a whole by his subservience to the Pope.

At the same time the Great Council was developing into a rudimentary Parliament. It had no legislative or executive power, but, sometimes reinforced by knights of the shire elected in the shire courts, it

The Temple Church, built by the Knights Templar in 1185 on the model of the round Church of the Holy Sepulchre, Jerusalem. It has been jointly occupied by the Inner and Middle Temple since the beginning of the Inns of Court.

Harlech Castle, one of the four castles built by Edward I to keep North Wales in subjection. It was originally on the coast but the sea has receded.

debated affairs of state and was beginning to claim some share in the government. By 1258 Simon de Montfort had become leader of the opposition, not, however, of his fellow barons, who were pursuing a selfish class policy, but of a new nationalist party that called for reform and England for the English – a significant demand. There followed a short civil war in which Henry was defeated, and in 1265 Simon, now virtually dictator, called a Parliament that included not only knights of the shire but burgesses from the towns that supported him. It was a momentous assembly, for it was the first time that the Commons had been represented.

A few months later Simon was killed at the Battle of Evesham, where Henry's son, Prince Edward, defeated him. The royal authority was restored, and Henry reigned peaceably until his death in 1272.

His son, Edward I, was every inch a king, strong both in body and mind, and because, like Simon de Montfort, he identified himself with the rising spirit of nationalism among his people, and had their support, he was able to check the encroachments of the barons and the Church. This he did by inquiring into baronial privileges, by preventing the multiplication of feudal overlords, and prohibiting gifts of land to the already overwealthy Church. He further advanced the royal

Seal of Simon de Montfort, 1258.

jurisdiction at the expense of the barons, and the Exchequer, Common Pleas and King's Bench became separate courts. He promoted trade, but showed the ugly side of nationalism by expelling the Jews.

To do these things he needed the support of the humbler classes of the nation, for now, for the first time, we may begin to speak of an English nation. The upper classes were beginning to learn the language of their inferiors, their younger sons were going into trade, and the sons of villeins were at the universities and scaling the hierarchy of the Church and law. They were even to be found in Parliament, as meet‑ings of the Great Council were coming to be called, and butchers, bakers, tailors, drapers sat with earls, knights, bishops and abbots in the Parliaments of Edward I. They did not wish to come, for Edward had no intention of allowing them any control; he merely wanted their money, though it was also desirable that they should agree to part with it, for 'what touches all,' he said, 'should be approved by all'. It was a maxim that was to have important consequences.

England was the first European country to be quickened by the spirit of nationalism; it had expressed itself in the expulsion of Henry III's foreign favourites and of the Jews, and now it was turned aggres‑sively against the other countries of the British Isles. The mountainous region of north and western Wales had never been subdued, but when Llewelyn led a Celtic rebellion Edward hunted down and destroyed him, and built castles to secure the new Principality. His eldest son was born at one of these, Carnarvon, and a few years later created the first Prince of Wales. The Principality was not incorporated in England, but was governed separately, and the eastern half of Wales was left to the feudal jurisdiction of the Marcher Lords.

The situation in Ireland was not unlike that in Wales before its conquest. The Pale round Dublin was administered like an English shire, but beyond that Anglo‑Irish feudalism petered out in the central bogs until in the far west Celtic tribal chiefs ruled unmolested. Edward did not undertake its conquest, but in his reign English power reached its highest point, and the country enjoyed an unaccustomed prosperity.

Scotland, too, was racially and geographically divided: into the Gaelic‑speaking Celtic tribes of the Highlands and the predominantly

Saxon and feudal Lowlands. A disputed succession to the throne gave Edward the chance of intervention, and in 1296 he invaded the country, defeated the Scots and triumphantly carried off the Stone of Scone on which their kings were crowned. But nationalism kindles nationalism, and Edward's aggression led only to rebellion under national heroes. Although the first, William Wallace, was defeated and barbarously executed in 1305, Scotland was not defeated; Robert Bruce was crowned, and under his leadership the struggle was continued.

This attempted conquest led to the long alliance of Scotland with France, one on either side of England, for Edward had become involved in war with the French king, who tried to seize his possessions in Gascony. It was these difficulties that made him summon the Model Parliament of 1295, in which the three estates of Barons, Clergy and Commons were represented, though this did not prevent his extortion of more than the customary export duty on wool to finance his campaigns. Edward's necessity was the baron's opportunity, and in 1297 they compelled him to sign a confirmation of Magna Carta with the additional clause that the king should not levy taxes in excess of the accustomed aids save 'by the common consent of the realm'. Parliament had asserted its right to control taxation.

While preparing to invade Scotland for the fourth time, Edward died near Carlisle, and the thirteenth century was over.

It was one of the great centuries in our history, a Plantagenet spring after the grim Norman winter, when the spirit of man began to unfold like the foliated capitals on the shafted columns of his churches, no longer sombre Romanesque but springing Gothic, the vital, aspiring Early English style. It was the century of the building of Salisbury Cathedral, when medieval sculpture and stained glass reached their perfection; of Roger Bacon and his friend Robert Grosseteste, Bishop of Lincoln; of the foundation of the universities and Inns of Court; the development of the Common Law; the evolution of Parliament; the creation of a social order that no longer denied but was buttressed by the liberty of the subject, however limited; the realization of unity, the discovery of the nation and the emergence of English as its language. Such a century, one of the most peaceful, may well be called one of the

Spinning in the late thirteenth century.

Seal of delivery of wool at Winchester in the reign of Edward I.

The Coronation Chair made for Edward I, containing the Stone of Scone on which Scottish kings used to be crowned.

A Parliament of Edward I.

greatest in our history, and what is perhaps the earliest English lyric, written in the middle of Henry III's reign, expresses its vernal expectancy:

> Sumer is icumen in,
> Lhude sing cuccu!
> Groweth sed, and bloweth med,
> And springth the wude nu –
> Sing cuccu!

It was a premature spring, however, and two centuries of war and discord were to pass before there was such another advance.

'Sumer is icumen in'–a six-men's song of unusual complexity for the thirteenth century.

Salisbury Cathedral, the supreme example of thirteenth-century, Early English, architecture.

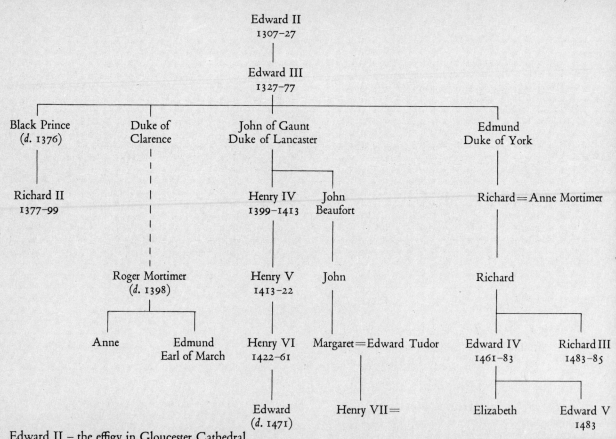

Edward II
1307–27

Edward III
1327–77

Black Prince
(*d.* 1376)

Duke of
Clarence

John of Gaunt
Duke of Lancaster

Edmund
Duke of York

Richard II
1377–99

Henry IV
1399–1413

John
Beaufort

Richard = Anne Mortimer

Roger Mortimer
(*d.* 1398)

Henry V
1413–22

John

Richard

Anne

Edmund
Earl of March

Henry VI
1422–61

Margaret = Edward Tudor

Edward IV
1461–83

Richard III
1483–85

Edward
(*d.* 1471)

Henry VII =

Elizabeth

Edward V
1483

Edward II – the effigy in Gloucester Cathedral.

Effigy of the Black Prince, 1330–76, in Canterbury Cathedral.

Edward I's shiftless and extravagant son, Edward II, a young man of twenty-three whose chief delight was in an upstart Gascon, Piers Gaveston, gave the barons their chance. In 1310 in a Parliament limited to themselves, they took over the government and murdered Gaveston. Their feudal forces, however, were unable to check Bruce, now beginning to threaten England, and in 1314 the Scots routed them at Bannockburn. Bruce thereupon ravaged northern England and sent a force to Ireland, which, in alliance with the Celtic chiefs, destroyed the country's brief prosperity and reduced English power to the limits of the Pale. Edward I's project of a united British Isles was in ruins, and an independent Scotland in alliance with France was to be a menace for more than two centuries, the period of border warfare celebrated in *Chevy Chase* and other ballads.

The brutality, selfishness and mismanagement of the baronial oligarchy rallied supporters round the king. At Boroughbridge the barons were defeated, and a full Parliament of 1322 declared their ordinances invalid because they had not been confirmed by the commonalty of the realm. Thus, the century-old attempt of the nobility to take over the central government ended in failure, and the next stage of the struggle would be to gain control of the Commons.

Edward's triumph did not last long. He was overthrown by his wife and her lover, and murdered.

The new king, young Edward III, had his grandfather's brawn without his brains. Self-indulgent, extravagant, with a passion for fighting, he was the very pattern of the bogus chivalry of the age, when knights were spared for their ransoms and the poor were slaughtered. It was an age of splendid pageantry, of the institution of the Order of the Garter and perfection of heraldic art, of superficial brilliance but of fundamental selfishness, greed, insincerity and brutality, an age without idealism. Perhaps it was a rapidly increasing prosperity, the result of the manufacture and export of woollen cloth, that led to this decline of spiritual values, and Edward was not slow to exploit the combination of nationalism and materialism in his subjects.

After an unsuccessful attempt to subjugate Scotland, he turned to a more profitable prey, rich and feudally impotent France, and in 1337 the Hundred Years' War began. This new venture, the first attempt of the English nation to expand beyond the British Isles, was popular

with all classes, or at least all freemen. For the burgesses it meant a market for their cloth, for the knights and other landowners a market for their wool, for the barons ransom from their captives, for the common soldiers booty, for the king glory, and perhaps the French crown which he claimed.

To support such a venture he needed money, and Parliament was prepared to supply it. In normal times the king was expected to manage with the revenue from his estates and law courts, from feudal dues and customary export duties, but war on this scale was something quite new, and Parliament was called upon to vote unprecedented supplies. This meant regular meetings and a steady increase in its power, particu-larly of the Commons, now beginning to sit separately from the barons in their own chamber, the chapter house of Westminster Abbey. The lower clergy gradually ceased to attend, and the House of Commons became entirely an assembly of laymen.

Chapter house, Westminster Abbey: the House of Commons from about 1300 to 1547.

The fourteenth-century house of William Grevel, the Cotswold wool merchant, at Chipping Campden.

J. ....
bal refconfit 7 refapen
toc mult mort 7 ocs. 7l

The Battle of Sluys, 1340, at the beginning of the Hundred Years' War. When Edward III claimed the throne of France, he also claimed sovereignty of the Channel, which he secured by this great naval victory, when he himself led the English fleet.

The first twenty years of the war were brilliantly successful. The victory of Edward and his longbowmen over the old-fashioned chivalry of France at Crécy in 1346 was followed by the similar victory of his eldest son, the Black Prince, at Poitiers ten years later; and when father and son had devastated whole provinces the French sued for peace and ceded Calais, Ponthieu and the whole of south-west France in full sovereignty.

That was in 1360. Twelve years earlier, however, England had suffered the fearful catastrophe of the Black Death, the plague that swept over Europe from the east. In 1348-9 almost every other person died, and the population was reduced from about four million to little more

than two. The economic and social consequences were disastrous: land went out of cultivation, prices rose, free labourers demanded higher wages and villeins who were still subject to the manor demanded their freedom. Their masters in Parliament, many of them also justices of the peace whom Edward had established to help the sheriff in local government, replied with statutes to keep down wages and prevent the emancipation of their serfs, measures that were to produce the first great labour upheaval thirty years later.

To this smouldering discontent was added resentment against the luxury and corruption of the Church: not against the parish priests, most of whom were poor and humble men, but against the hunting

The Black Death, 1348–9, which killed nearly half the people of England and brought about great economic and political unrest.

'Lamentable, savage and violent.' An inscription of 1350 on the wall of Ashwell church, Hertfordshire, describing the Black Death.

A Canterbury Pilgrim: the Monk.

Of priking and of hunting for the hare
Was al his lust, for no cost wolde he spare

The Wycliffe Bible. The English translation made by John Wycliffe, 'the morning star of the Reformation' (c. 1329–84), and his followers. This is the beginning of the *Acts of the Apostles*.

monks, wanton friars and traffickers in pardons from the Pope, or rather a Pope, for after 1377 there was one in Rome and a competitor in Avignon. This resentment was voiced by John Wycliffe and his followers, the Lollards, precursors of the Reformation, who denounced the Pope and the superstitious practices of the day.

Meanwhile the war had been renewed, and with it the crippling taxation of an impoverished people to finance the futile ravaging and murderous raids of Edward's sons, the Black Prince and John of Gaunt. Edward himself was in the arms of his mistress, by 1373 the Black Prince was dying, and the virtual ruler of the country was John of Gaunt, Duke of Lancaster.

There were no dukes in England until Edward created the Black Prince Duke of Cornwall; now all his sons were royal dukes, who by marriages with heiresses had absorbed innumerable earldoms. The nobility had shrunk and changed its character; the Norman nobility had been a large class of comparatively small barons and a few earls, now they were a small class of immensely powerful men, with John of Gaunt in control of a Parliament packed with his own supporters.

Edward died in 1377, and all that remained of his former French conquest was Calais and a few towns on the west coast.

John of Gaunt continued the war on behalf of his nephew, Richard II, who was only eleven, and Parliament sanctioned a poll-tax on every male over the age of sixteen. It was the last straw, and in 1381 the peasants all over the country rose spontaneously, demanding repeal of the tax and abolition of villeinage. Some marched on London, where the citizens supported them; John of Gaunt's palace of the Savoy was sacked and the Archbishop murdered, and it was only the courage of the boy king that prevented further destruction. By promising to redress their grievances he persuaded them to disperse; but once the danger was over, the government ignored his promises and hanged the leaders.

Richard II's reign has obvious resemblances to that of Edward II. The so-called Lords Appellant, led by his uncle Gloucester and his cousin Henry Bolingbroke, John of Gaunt's son, packed Parliament and secured the execution or exile of his friends. They overreached themselves, however, and Richard was able to assert his authority. Nine years he waited, then in 1397 he struck. The Appellants were arrested and found guilty of conspiracy by a Parliament packed this time by Richard, and Gloucester was murdered and Henry exiled. Then, when John of Gaunt died, Richard seized all the vast estates of the Duchy of Lancaster. Now it was Richard who had overreached himself; his despotic actions so estranged his supporters that when Henry returned to claim his inheritance Richard had to surrender and sign a deed of abdication.

In Westminster Hall, when Parliament had formally deposed Richard on the charge of violating his coronation oath, Henry rose and spoke in English: 'In the name of Fadir Son and Holy Ghost, I Henry of Lancaster chalenge this Rewme of Ingland and the Corone,' and the Archbishop led him by the hand to the empty throne. Thus did the Commons, now a pawn in the hands of rival court factions, first depose a king and elect another. A few months later Richard died in prison.

The Peasants' Revolt, 1381. Wat Tyler, leader of the Kentish rebels, threatens Richard II with his sword but the Mayor of London intervenes.

The decline of standards in the fourteenth century is reflected in its art. Although sometimes very beautiful, the Decorated Gothic of the period is often over-decorated, over-pretty, and the figures in the stained glass windows are characteristically a monotonous series of saints or soldiers standing in the same affected attitude under identical elaborate canopies.

Yet the century can boast one great glory: the triumph of the English tongue. Latin was the language of the learned clergy, and since the Conquest French had been that of the upper classes, English being confined virtually to the peasants. In the course of three hundred years these lowly, illiterate folk had so simplified it, shedding its elaborate inflections, that it now emerged as a wonderfully flexible medium enriched with the graces of Latin and French. The English nation was in the middle of a war with France, and in 1362 English replaced French as the language of the law courts, and by 1385 'in alle the gramere scoles of Engelond, children leveth Frensche and construeth and lerneth in Englische', so that they 'conneth no more Frensche than can thir left heele'.

These were the years when Geoffrey Chaucer was growing up, and the result was the first great poetry in our language. The worldly Chaucer was not a reformer like Wycliffe, translator of the Bible, nor a fanatic like Langland, whose *Piers Plowman* was a defence of the poor and denunciation of abuses, but on reading the *Canterbury Tales* one feels that in spite of the abuses, the greedy monks and merciless bullies at the top, the English people as a whole were fundamentally sound. And the popular drama, the miracle plays performed by guilds of master craftsmen, reinforces this impression of vigorous life. Freedom was in the air, for despite the efforts of their masters to repress them, villeins were rapidly gaining their liberty, and it is significant that of Chaucer's twenty-nine Canterbury pilgrims one was a yeoman.

We have now reached the period covered by the great sequence of Shakespeare's history plays, which demonstrates the discord that follows the violent overthrow of established order, and its resolution only after many years of conflict. In Norman times the barons had tried to make themselves semi-independent feudal rulers, in the thirteenth century they

Henry IV, who supplanted his cousin Richard II, thus becoming first of the Lancastrian kings, 1399–1413.

had tried to seize control of the central government, in the fourteenth they gained control of the House of Commons, and now, at the beginning of the fifteenth one of their number had gained the crown itself. Lancaster had supplanted Plantagenet.

Henry IV's position was precarious, however. He was king by conquest and election, not by heredity, for the real heir was the boy Edmund Mortimer, Earl of March, descended from an elder brother of John of Gaunt. For this reason Henry had to submit to Parliament, which was tantamount to submission to the peers, who thus increased their power over the crown, as well as their own power by enlisting private armies of retainers. To conciliate the Church Henry agreed to the atrocious statute *De Heretico Comburendo* directed against the Lollards, so beginning religious persecution and the burning of heretics.

All his subservience, however, did not prevent rebellions, the most formidable being that of the Percies of Northumberland in alliance with the Scots and Welsh under Owen Glendower. Though the rebels were defeated, for the remaining years of his reign Henry could never feel secure.

Geoffrey Chaucer, *c.* 1340-1400.

The poet Thomas Hoccleve presents his *Regiment of Princes* to Prince Henry, the future Henry V, *c.* 1410.

A fifteenth-century siege, of the time of the Hundred Years' War.

His son Henry V was an equally devout persecutor of the Lollards, and even his former friend, Sir John Oldcastle, the original of Falstaff, was 'hanged and brent on the galous'. Then, to divert attention from his tenuous claim to the crown, he busied 'giddy minds in foreign quarrels' and, cynically renewing the even more tenuous claim to the French crown, invaded France, already distracted by civil war. After the brilliant victory at Agincourt in 1415 he was able to dictate terms of peace, whereby he married the daughter of the imbecile French king and was recognized as his heir.

Two years later both he and the French king died, leaving the crowns of both countries to the infant Henry VI. This monstrous arrangement united the feudally divided French against England, and a new nationalism was inspired by Joan of Arc, who drove the hated 'goddams' out of Champagne and its capital Reims, where the Dauphin was crowned. Joan was betrayed to the English and burned as a witch, but her spirit lived on, and by 1453 the only possession left in English hands was Calais. The Hundred Years' War in France was over, but only to be followed by a thirty years' war in England, the Wars of the Roses.

During the minority of Henry VI, while France was being lost, Parliament steadily advanced its power, obtaining the right to draw up Bills, instead of mere petitions, for the king's assent, and limiting the electors of the Commons to forty shilling freeholders. Two rival factions were now struggling for its control: on the one hand the Lancastrians, led by the Beaufort descendants of John of Gaunt, and Margaret, Henry's queen, Henry himself having inherited the weak mind of his French grandfather: on the other the Yorkists, led by the Duke of York, who through his mother inherited the Mortimer claim to the throne, and the Earl of Warwick, the most powerful subject in England.

In 1453 Margaret bore Henry a son, and two years later the civil war broke out: the Red Rose of Lancaster against the White Rose of York. It was a war of naked selfishness and pitiless ferocity, symbolized in the last two parts of Shakespeare's *Henry VI* by the imagery drawn from flint, traps, snakes, tigers, wolves and other beasts of prey, and each party celebrated its victories by the wholesale execution of its captives, 'legalized' by a Parliament packed with its supporters.

After a skirmish at St Albans, when York captured the crazy king, the main battles in the first phase of the war were the Lancastrian victory at Wakefield, where York was captured and murdered, followed in 1461 by the Yorkist triumph at Towton, shortly before which Warwick had secured the crowning of the new Duke of York as Edward IV. After his victory the Commons thanked him for assuming the crown as Richard II's true heir, and denounced the Lancastrians

as usurpers. There were the usual executions, and the wretched Henry VI was thrown into the Tower. York had supplanted Lancaster.

York had also supplanted Parliament. Many of the nobles who had controlled it had been killed in battle or murdered or executed, and their estates and revenues now enriched the crown. Edward IV, therefore, was no longer dependent on Parliament for money, and its premature period of power was over. It was just as well, for, as it had been constituted, it had been a major cause of disorder.

The Tower of London in the fifteenth century, where so many princes perished during the Wars of the Roses.

An apprentice or journeyman mason and carpenter examined by the Guild Warden before being admitted master craftsmen.

But although Edward could dispense with Parliament, he owed his crown to Warwick, and in those faithless times it was inevitable that the next stage of the struggle should be between king and kingmaker. By marrying a desirable widow of no great rank and aggrandizing her family, Edward offended Warwick, who now joined forces with Queen Margaret, but in 1471 he was killed at Barnet, and a month later Margaret's army was routed at Tewkesbury. Her son, Prince Edward, was captured and killed, and her husband, Henry VI,

77

murdered in the Tower. Only one Lancastrian claimant to the throne was left, Henry Tudor, Earl of Richmond, son of a Welsh knight who had married Margaret Beaufort; but he was only a schoolboy living in France.

For the moment Edward had nothing to fear from the Lancastrians, and the struggle now narrowed to one of York against York. His two younger brothers, the Dukes of Clarence and Gloucester, were quarrelling over the Warwick spoils, both had an eye on the crown, and Clarence, who had at one time joined the Lancastrians, was accused of treason and sent to the Tower where he was murdered. How far Gloucester was responsible is unknown.

Edward was now in more senses than one the true heir of Richard II, for he had achieved the despotism that Richard had tried to attain; but he had also restored some sort of temporary order, and for that at least he deserved his popularity with the London citizens and their wives, in whose society he delighted. He did not live long to enjoy it; sinking back into sloth and self-indulgence, he died in 1483.

He was succeeded by the elder of his two young sons, Edward V, a boy of twelve, with his uncle Gloucester as Protector. But Gloucester intended to be king. He got rid of Edward's supporters, asserted that the young king was illegitimate, and Parliament was persuaded to crown him, instead of his nephew, as Richard III. Soon afterwards the two young princes were murdered in the Tower.

This was the signal for the final act of the civil war. In 1485 Henry Tudor, now a man of twenty-six, landed at Milford Haven and marched through Wales, where many of his countrymen joined him. At Bosworth in Leicestershire the last battle was fought; Richard was killed and Henry crowned on the scene of his victory. The Wars of the Roses were over, and the discord that had begun with the deposition and murder of Richard II was resolved when Lancaster and York were united by Henry VII's marriage with Edward IV's daughter Elizabeth, a reconciliation symbolized by the red and white rose of the House of Tudor.

This century of foreign war and civil war, of corrupt clergy and rapacious princes, had produced no great men, and progress had been

The Chapel of King's College, Cambridge. Built mainly by Henry VI, it is the finest of all buildings in the Perpendicular Gothic style.

material rather than spiritual, notably the development of woollen manufacture and foreign trade. There was no English poet comparable to Chaucer, and it is significant that the greatest literary work of the period, *Morte d'Arthur*, was a prose romance of the chivalry of the Round Table written in prison by a Yorkist knight, Sir Thomas Malory, guilty of theft, extortion, rape, and at least attempted murder. Yet all over the country new churches were going up and old ones being enlarged in the delicate Perpendicular Gothic peculiar to England, symbol perhaps of its insular nationalism and presage of a national religion.

'We will unite the white rose and the red.' The double Tudor Rose of Henry VII, symbolizing the reconciliation of York and Lancaster.

Book Two

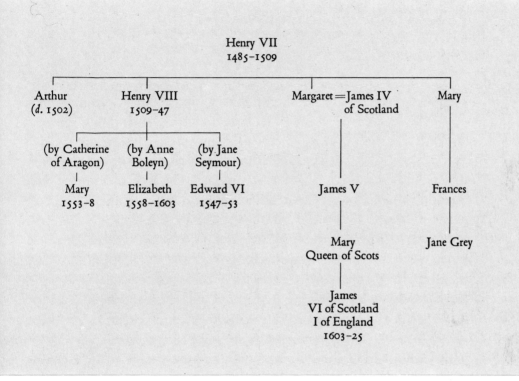

Henry VII
1485–1509

Arthur
(d. 1502)

Henry VIII
1509–47

Margaret ═ James IV
of Scotland

Mary

(by Catherine
of Aragon)

(by Anne
Boleyn)

(by Jane
Seymour)

Mary
1553–8

Elizabeth
1558–1603

Edward VI
1547–53

James V

Frances

Mary
Queen of Scots

Jane Grey

James
VI of Scotland
I of England
1603–25

When Henry VII wrested the crown from Richard III the Middle Ages were almost over. The medieval social and economic order was breaking down. Most of the villeins had been freed and become either wage labourers or yeomen, paid servants of some lord or small independent farmers, and a capitalist system of manufacture was replacing the guild system, men and women being employed in their homes to spin and weave the material supplied by its owner. Although the medieval state was by no means a welfare state, at least manor and guild were

7
*Renaissance,
Reformation
and a New
World
1485–1603*

in some sort responsible for their members, but medieval collectivism was now giving place to individualism.

Moreover, the old nobility had almost destroyed itself in thirty years of internecine war – there was only one duke left at the end of Henry VII's reign – and the lord of the manor was now typically a country gentleman and justice of the peace living quietly on the outskirts of a village in an unfortified manor house. In any event the new invention of gunpowder made fortifications almost as useless as the plate armour worn by knights in the late wars, and the king was the only man who could afford a train of cannon.

Feudalism, dependence on a local magnate, had been superseded by nationalism, loyalty to the king and his central government, not only in England, but to some degree in France, Spain and Portugal (Germany and Italy were to wait nearly another four centuries), and while Henry VII was consolidating his power, Columbus was planting the Spanish flag in America, and Portuguese adventurers were doubling the Cape of Good Hope on their way to India. The little medieval world of western Europe, of which England had been the unprofitable fringe, was expanding into a globe on which she was a promontory thrust out towards a New World.

Even more important, perhaps, than these geographical discoveries was the rediscovery of Greek civilization and consequent expansion of man's spirit which we call the Renaissance: the Rebirth of Learning and of free inquiry, the revolt against authority, the exaltation of the individual, of the mind and body, of life, instead of the medieval preoccupation with the soul and death. It was the art of Greece that enchanted the Italians, but for the northerner Greek meant the language of the New Testament, and by 1497 John Colet was lecturing at Oxford on St Paul's Epistles and sweeping away the accumulated rubbish of medieval scholasticism. It was a short step to criticism of the medieval church, and as Dean of St Paul's he denounced the ignorance, worldliness and greed of the monks and higher clergy. It was the abuses, not the doctrine of the Church that he attacked, and in this he was supported by his friends, Dutch Erasmus and young Thomas More, and for that matter most of his countrymen.

Henry VII, first of the Tudors, 1485–1509.

Then, just at this critical period of intellectual ferment came the means of disseminating the new ideas. In 1477 William Caxton set up his printing press in Westminster, and in the Preface to his first printed book wrote: 'It is not wreton with penne and ynke as other bokes ben . . . for all the bookes of this storye named the Recule of the Historyes of Troyes thus enpryntid as ye here see were begonne in oon day, and also fynysshid in oon day.' A hundred years before, the hopeless ambition of Chaucer's Oxford scholar had been to have a library of twenty books.

Of course this physical and spiritual expansion had little immediate effect on the great majority of the four million people of England, for whom life flowed on much as it had done in their fathers' time, but it is clear enough to us that they were living at the beginning of an unprecedentedly exciting age.

Henry's mission was to bring peace and order to a distracted country, and his instrument was the Privy Council, which was to become the main governing body of the Tudors. In its judicial capacity it was represented by the Court of Star Chamber, too powerful to be overawed, which put an end to private armies of liveried retainers. It was a dangerous precedent, however, for the Court was independent of the Common Law, though this was preserved by the unpaid justices of the peace who administered it locally, who were in fact, and were to remain, the local government until the creation of borough and county councils in the nineteenth century. Parliament was a very different assembly from what it had been; a chastened and depleted House of Lords and a Commons composed of duly elected knights of the shire and burgesses, it was occasionally called to assent to new laws and vote taxes, though the frugal Henry had little need of extra money. He had plenty of his own, and instead of indulging in foreign wars he encouraged foreign trade and sought foreign alliances.

His daughter Margaret he married to James IV of Scotland, and his elder son Arthur to Catherine of Aragon, daughter of the King of Spain. This was a particularly prudent match. Spain was the rival of France, the traditional enemy of England; moreover, the Netherlands were now a Spanish province and the greater part of English trade

Caxton presenting his translation of the *Tales of Troy*, the first book that he printed, to Margaret of York, sister of Edward IV, and wife of the Duke of Burgundy.

went through the port of Antwerp. Arthur's death in 1502, therefore, was unfortunate, but Henry persuaded the Pope to allow him to transfer the bride to his younger son, another Henry.

As a Lancastrian, he had inevitably his troubles with the remaining Yorkists. There was Lambert Simnel who claimed to be the son of Clarence, and Perkin Warbeck who was said to be the younger of the princes murdered in the Tower. But when Henry died in 1509 the Yorkist cause was dead, and he left his heir a peaceful and united country and a brimming treasury.

The heir, Henry VIII, was a boy of eighteen with all the gifts of Fortune. Athlete, poet, musician and patron of the arts and the New Learning, his court was that of a Renaissance prince. The poets Skelton, Surrey and Wyatt were there, and Holbein and Sir Thomas More, who in 1516 published his *Utopia*, with its protests against sheep enclosure by greedy landlords and the ferocious punishment of crime.

The young king was as impetuous as his father had been cautious, and, ambitious to emulate the exploits of Henry V a hundred years before, invaded France. ('They detest war as a very brutal thing', More was writing of his Utopians, 'which, to the reproach of human nature, is more practised by men than by any sort of beasts. They think that there is nothing more inglorious than that glory which is gained by war.') But Henry gained no glory, though in his absence the invading Scots had been disastrously defeated at Flodden, and he prudently withdrew to spend his money on a royal navy.

The man who had encouraged Henry's extravagant foreign adventures was Thomas Wolsey, Archbishop of York, Cardinal and Chancellor. Proud, of limitless ambition and almost as rich as the king, he was the very type of prelate denounced by Colet and More. Yet he was princely in his spending; he enlarged his London palace of York Place, built Hampton Court farther up the river, and anticipated Henry's foundation of Trinity College, Cambridge, by founding Cardinal College, later Christ Church, at Oxford. But he was the most unpopular man in England, and the days of his triumph were numbered.

Sir Thomas More, Lord Chancellor and his family. A sketch by Holbein, perhaps to commemorate More's fiftieth birthday in 1528. On his right is his father, Sir John More, on his left his only son, John.

By 1527 Henry was thirty-six, Catherine forty-two, yet their only surviving child was a daughter, Mary, and Henry wanted a son – and he also wanted Anne Boleyn. Convinced, therefore, that his marriage with his brother's widow was unlawful, he ordered Wolsey to obtain the Pope's confirmation of its invalidity. In the normal way the Pope would have obliged, but he was in the power of the King of Spain, Catherine's nephew, and had to refuse. Wolsey's failure was his downfall, but he died in 1530 before he could be executed on a charge of high treason. He was replaced as the king's chief adviser by Thomas Cromwell, and Henry moved into York Place, renamed Whitehall, the old Palace of Westminster having recently been burned down.

The long struggle of the English kings against the power of the Pope had come to a head. Henry had no sympathy with those who wished to change Catholic doctrine, but he was determined to escape from papal interference. The Parliament that he called for this purpose supported him, and in the seven years that it sat it recovered much of its former importance.

After some preliminary skirmishing, in 1534 it passed the Act of Supremacy, declaring the king to be 'Supreme Head of the Church of England'. Meanwhile, Archbishop Cranmer had pronounced Henry's marriage with Catherine invalid, Henry had married Anne Boleyn, and in 1533 the Princess Elizabeth was born. The Pope replied by excommunicating Henry and declaring him deposed, but Henry, now head of the Church as well as the state, could afford to laugh at his opponent, for he was more powerful than any of his predecessors had been.

He was soon to become even more powerful. The Church owned a quarter of the country, and Henry was in need of money. Cromwell was ordered to suppress the monasteries, and within a few years their enormous wealth was transferred to the king. A little was devoted to the endowment of new bishoprics, but the great bulk went into the empty treasury, the confiscated estates and buildings being sold to speculators and others with money to invest. In this way the property of the Church passed into the hands of a new nobility and gentry who,

Lacock Abbey, Wiltshire. Originally a nunnery, at the Dissolution of the Monasteries it was acquired by Sir William Sharington, who converted it into a house *c.* 1540. His octagonal tower remains, but most of his work was altered between 1750 and 1830.

though they probably cared not a straw about religion, now had a vested interest in supporting this first phase of the Reformation.

There was trouble, of course, and the Yorkshire rising known as the Pilgrimage of Grace was savagely suppressed. Henry was more successful in dealing with his own countrymen than with the northerners, and in 1535 united Wales with England on equal terms. It was the first Act of Union in the history of Britain, which would have been very different had England had a line of Irish as well as Welsh and Scottish kings.

The dissolution of the monas-teries, however, was generally acceptable as a fulfilment of popular anti-clerical feeling, and it is impor-tant to remember that this first stage of the Reformation was purely political, involving no change of doctrine. Henry was Defender of the Faith, his Act of Six Articles decreed death for those who questioned transubstantiation or clerical celibacy, and he burned im-partially both Protestants and those Catholics who refused to accept his Anglican revolution. To empha-size the national character of his Church, the service was to be in English instead of Latin, and every

Henry VIII, 1509–47.

Cardinal Wolsey, 1471?–1530.

89

parish church was to have an English Bible. This was the 'Great Bible' of 1539, mainly the work of Miles Coverdale, who based his translation on the version of William Tyndale, a reformer burned abroad as a heretic. In this way some of the noblest prose in the language became the common heritage of the English people, and encouraged a freedom of thought and devotion to the Anglican Church that eased the way for the next stage of the Reformation.

There was little enough to encourage devotion to the supreme head of the Church. Power had corrupted the splendid prince of the early years into a bloodthirsty tyrant who rid himself of all who thwarted his will, even Sir Thomas More, who was unable to accept the Act of Supremacy, even Cromwell, even Anne Boleyn and her suspected lovers.

The day after Anne's execution Henry married Jane Seymour. She died a year later in childbirth, but the child was a son, the only direct heir to the throne, for both the princesses, Mary and Elizabeth, had been declared illegitimate, and though Henry had three more wives there were no more children. All depended, therefore, on the delicate but precocious Prince Edward, and to secure the succession and unite the whole island Henry proposed his betrothal to his sister's grand-daughter, the infant Queen of Scots. The proposal was ill-received by the Scottish nobility, and Henry's wooing was with the sword. This

William Tyndale's version was the basis of the 'Great Bible'. This is Tyndale's translation of the beginning of *Corinthians I*, chapter 13.

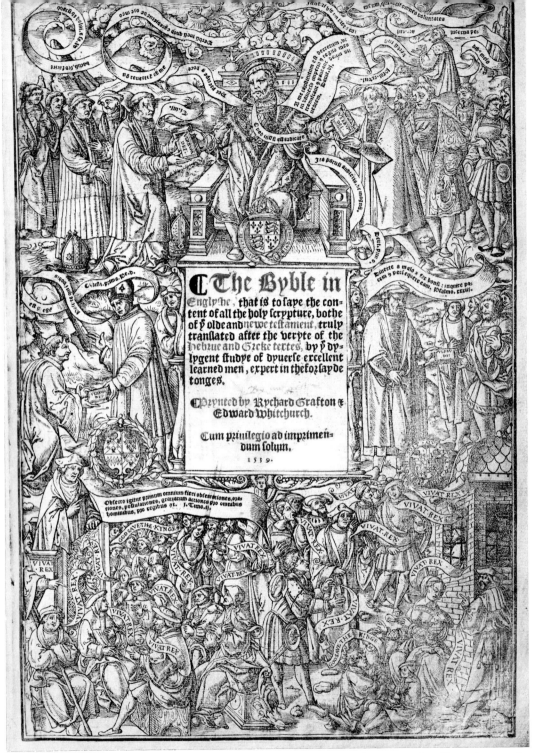

The Great Bible of 1539. Henry VIII gives the Word of God to his bishops and nobles, who pass it on to the common people who cry 'God save the Kynge!' and 'Vivat Rex!'

involved another futile and costly war with France, to finance which Henry debased the currency, so adding another problem for his successor.

He died in 1547, a few days after he had sent the young poet Earl of Surrey to the block. He was a gross and selfish tyrant, yet he worked through Parliament, servile though it often was, and he loved his country, which he left a more truly united and confident nation than ever before; and a reign that produced the Utopian vision of More, the drawings of Holbein, the poetry of Wyatt and music of Cornyshe has other claims to greatness.

There followed a disastrous decade, a violent oscillation impelled by greed and fanaticism, out to an extreme Protestantism and back to a medieval Catholicism. Discord in religion and its exploitation for political ends were now to make the creation of order still more difficult. The Defender of the Faith had kept the forces of religious change severely in check, but Edward VI was only nine, and his uncle the Protector Somerset, a liberal-minded doctrinaire, was himself a Protestant. The ferocious persecuting measures were repealed, and Protestant preachers, the most influential of whom was the lovable Hugh Latimer, were soon converting the people, particularly in London and the neighbouring counties. Then in 1549 Cranmer, who was moving towards Protestantism, issued his English Prayer Book which an Act of Uniformity ordered to be used in churches instead of the Latin service.

Meanwhile the country's economy was deteriorating. The debasement of the currency had sent prices soaring, trade was in confusion, and the treasury was empty. But Henry had not relieved the Church of all its superfluous wealth; the endowments of chantries and religious guilds remained. Somerset seized these, though much of the plunder went to enrich himself and the gentry at the expense of education, as Latimer boldly protested. Indeed, the number of schools was reduced, for those attached to the guilds were suppressed, and the so-called Edward VI Grammar Schools were merely those which, like the one at Stratford, were re-established. At the same time the enclosure of land for sheep-rearing by the businesslike gentry led to serious unemployment, for pasture land needs far less labour than arable.

The country was seething with discontent, the people of the backward and conservative west and north being particularly enraged by the rapid religious changes and wanton destruction of images and stained glass in their churches. As a result there were two formidable risings in 1549, the Prayer Book rebellion in Cornwall and Devon, and Kett's insurrection against enclosure in Norfolk. Both were suppressed, but Somerset was discredited and replaced by John Dudley, Duke of Northumberland.

Northumberland had no religious convictions, but Protestantism meant profit for him and his like, and under his direction the churches were stripped of the poor remains of their property and left with little but a chalice and a single bell. Stone altars of the Mass were carried out and wooden tables for Communion carried in; priests were allowed to marry, a second Prayer Book was introduced, and non-attendance at church made punishable by fine or imprisonment.

Northumberland's position depended on his influence over the young king, now a fanatical Protestant, but the precocious boy was dying, and the next heir was either Mary Queen of Scots or Mary Tudor, both Catholics. He therefore married one of his sons to Lady Jane Grey, another great-granddaughter of Henry VII, and persuaded Edward to make a will in her favour. But when Edward died in 1553 the country would have nothing to do with Northumberland and his

The title page of the First English Prayer Book, 1549. An Act of Uniformity ordered this to be used instead of the Latin Service.

The burning at Oxford of Ridley and Latimer,
Bishops of London and Worcester, 16 October
1555. Cranmer *(top right)* awaits his turn.

Queen Mary, a fanatical Catholic, 1553–58.

daughter-in-law. Protestantism was associated with greed, corruption, misgovernment and distress, and Catholic Mary, daughter of the Spanish Catherine of Aragon, was joyfully acclaimed, even in largely Protestant London.

Mary, a woman of thirty-seven, forthright and inflexible, felt herself called by God to save England from the abomination of heresy, and England as a whole had no great objection to a return to the position

at the end of Henry VIII's reign, a Catholic country independent of Rome. But Mary was determined to return to the position at the beginning of her father's reign, and to this end agreed to marry Philip II of Spain. The Kentishmen rose in protest, but by the end of 1554 England had a Spanish king and was once again subject to the Pope.

It remained to persuade the Protestants of their error. The act *De Heretico Comburendo* was revived, and the burnings began. First the bishops: Hooper at Gloucester, Ridley and Latimer at Oxford, and in 1556 Cranmer. Then the humbler folk. Altogether some three hundred perished in the flames, old and young, women as well as men, but not those who had made their fortunes out of the spoliation of the Church. The snug gentry had no mind to martyrdom and no intention of surrendering their estates.

Latimer's last words to Ridley were prophetic: 'We shall this day light such a candle by God's grace in England as, I trust, shall never be put out.' The fires of Smithfield, where most of the victims suffered, secured the triumph of Protestantism in England. Even in that brutal age, so insensitive to suffering, the English people were revolted by the almost daily burnings, and in the following years John Foxe's *Book of Martyrs* was to become almost as influential as the Bible.

But the burnings were not the only cause of English anger — far worse horrors were being perpetrated in the name of religion in the Netherlands. Ten years before, England had been a proud and independent nation, now she was little better than a province of Spain subject to the Pope. France was the traditional enemy, but now it was Spain with its detested Inquisition, and the final humiliation came when England was dragged by Spain into a war with France that led only to the loss of Calais. No wonder that when Mary died in November 1558, hated, unhappy, but passionately convinced that she had done her best for her people, they danced and feasted in the streets of London and drank to the health of the new queen.

Elizabeth, a young woman of twenty-five, succeeded to a perilous heritage. The country was poor, weak, divided against itself, and surrounded by powerful enemies. Spain possessed the Netherlands and France controlled Scotland, where the French mother of the sixteen-year-old Mary Queen of Scots was Regent, and for all true Catholics Elizabeth was illegitimate and Mary the rightful Queen of England. Yet Elizabeth was equal to the situation; she had the Tudor courage, and combined an almost masculine intelligence with an altogether feminine intuition, which enabled her to understand her people and select the right advisers. Chief of these was William Cecil, Lord Burghley, who served her devotedly until his death forty years later.

Queen Elizabeth I, 1558–1603.

William Cecil, Lord Burghley, Elizabeth's
principal minister until his death in 1598.

Elizabeth's policy was one of compromise and delay, but a settle-ment of the religious question was urgent. She herself had no strong religious convictions; for her the matter was primarily a political one, and she aimed at a compromise that would unite as many of her people as possible. Parliament was called, and relations with Rome were severed again by a less provocative Act of Supremacy, and a slightly modified Prayer Book was reintroduced. The settlement was acceptable to all but the most zealous Catholics and extreme Protestants, or Puritans, as they were coming to be called.

In Scotland the extreme Protestants had their way. Under John Knox they revolted against the French army of occupation, and by the end of 1559 were besieging it in Leith. Knox appealed to Elizabeth, and an English fleet and army helped the Scots to expel the French for ever. It was an astonishing revolution. In 1558 England had been a Catholic country subject to Spain, and Scotland a Catholic country subject to France; by 1560 both had shaken off the yoke and had national Protestant Churches, the one episcopal, the other presbyterian. Moreover, France was soon involved in a civil war that reduced her to impotence for generations. Spain was the only danger.

Elizabeth and Cecil could now turn to reconstruction. In medieval times agriculture and industry had been regulated locally, but now that manor and guild no longer looked after the people it was essential that the state should take over their functions. By the Statute of Artificers all craftsmen were to serve a seven years' apprenticeship under a master, who was responsible for their welfare as well as their tuition. The enforcement of the Act was entrusted to the justices of the peace, the local gentry, who were empowered to fix wages in their districts. They were also responsible for levying a rate from the parish for relief of the

The *Ark Royal*, flagship of Lord Admiral Howard at the time of the Armada. She was a four-master of 800 tons and carried 425 men.

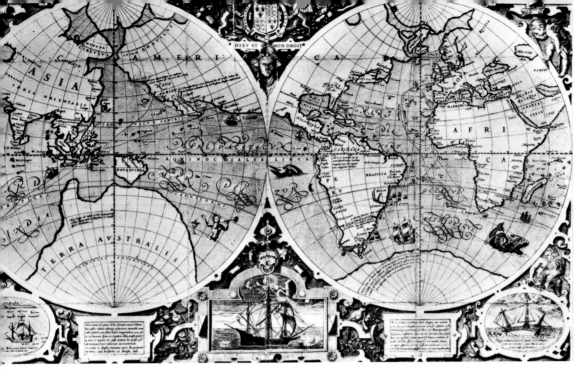

Map showing the circumnavigation of the world
by Francis Drake (1577–80)
and Thomas Cavendish (1586–88).

poor, and some attempt was made to find work for the unemployed. But the restoration of the coinage and consequent expansion of manufacture and trade eased, though they did not end, the unemployment problem, and by 1568, ten years after Elizabeth's accession, England was on the highroad to prosperity.

This was the year in which Francis Drake, aged twenty-three, made his first voyage to the New World with John Hawkins, who was selling African slaves to the Spaniards in the Caribbean, and the year in which Mary Queen of Scots was expelled from her country after marrying her husband's murderer. Leaving her baby son behind as King James VI, she sought refuge in England; an embarrassing guest, for Elizabeth could scarcely force her back on the Scottish people, and the only thing was to keep her in close confinement.

The next twenty years were a period of Catholic intrigue and Spanish plot to substitute Mary for Elizabeth as Queen: a period of cold war with Spain, for Elizabeth knew that England was not yet strong enough to risk an open breach with the power that dominated both Europe and the New World. In 1569 the semi-feudal northern earls rebelled; in 1570 the Pope excommunicated Elizabeth and released her Catholic subjects from their allegiance; in 1571 there was a conspiracy to marry the Duke of Norfolk to Mary, who was to become Queen. Norfolk was executed, last of the surviving English dukes.

Meanwhile Drake was engaged in his patriotic piracy, raiding the West Indies and sailing round the world to return laden with Spanish plunder. Elizabeth herself was flirting with her favourite, the Earl of Leicester, who entertained her royally at Kenilworth. The great country houses were going up – Longleat, Burghley, Montacute – and so were the first public theatres in London; Nicholas Hilliard, the successor of Holbein, was appointed painter to the Queen; in 1575 Thomas Tallis and William Byrd published a book of their motets dedicated to Elizabeth; Thomas Morley was transforming the religious motet into the secular madrigal, and advancing the golden age of English music; Philip Sidney was writing his *Arcadia* and sonnets to Stella and in 1579 Edmund Spenser published his *Shepherd's Calendar*. The decade of the '70s was the early spring of the Elizabethan Age, the spontaneous upsurge of the creative spirit, the triumphant expression of a united and confident people prepared for any adventure.

The crisis came in the next decade. The Spanish ambassador was involved in a plot to murder Elizabeth and expelled from the country, and two years later Mary herself was implicated in a similar conspiracy. Parliament and Privy Council demanded her death; Elizabeth reluctantly agreed, and at the beginning of 1587 she was executed.

The trial and execution of Mary Queen of Scots, 1587.

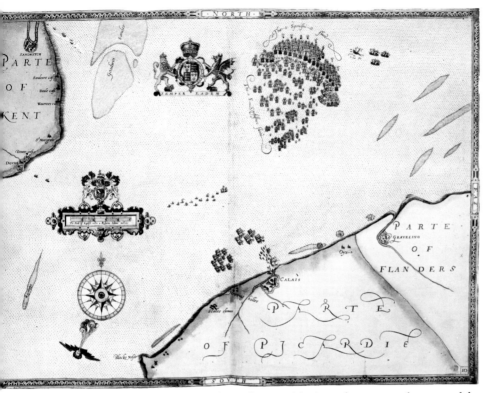

Driven out of Calais Roads by fireships, the Spanish Armada runs north, pursued by the English fleet, July 1588.

The twenty years' war with Spain had begun without any official declaration. Philip II was preparing to invade England from the Netherlands, and Elizabeth sent a small force under Leicester to support the revolt of the Dutch Protestants against their Spanish oppressors. It was on this ill-managed campaign that Sidney was mortally wounded, but the disaster was partly redeemed by the raid on Cadiz, where Drake disabled a great part of Philip's invasion fleet. Mary's execution, Sidney's death and Drake's raid all took place in 1587, and England awaited the fateful year 1588.

The attempted invasion came in July, but the lumbering galleons of Philip's great Armada were as helpless against the nimble English ships as the French chivalry had been against the English longbowmen at Agincourt. It was defeated by the new tactic of the broadside, and broken by a storm that drove it round the British Isles. The English lost one ship; less than half of the 'Invincible' Armada returned to Spain.

It was indeed an 'admirable year', as the prophets had foretold. England was now mistress of the seas, and the New World lay open to her adventurers, men like Raleigh, who was already trying to plant a colony in Virginia; and it was probably in this year that Shakespeare arrived in London and saw Marlowe's first play, *Tamburlaine*, which voiced the heroic aspirations of the new men of the Renaissance:

> Nature that framed us of four elements,
> Warring within our breasts for regiment,
> Doth teach us all to have aspiring minds:
> Our souls, whose faculties can comprehend
> The wondrous architecture of the world.

Medal of Elizabeth I, by Nicholas Hilliard, struck after the defeat of the Armada in 1588.

And measure every wandering planet's course,
Still climbing after knowledge infinite,
And always moving as the restless spheres,
Will us to wear ourselves, and never rest
Until we reach the ripest fruit of all.

The Spanish war dragged on for the rest of the reign, a desultory affair in which the English waylaid Spanish argosies and helped the Protestants of the Netherlands and France. In the 1590s Grenville was killed in the fight of the *Revenge*, Drake died while raiding the Spanish Main, in 1598 Elizabeth lost her faithful counsellor Burghley, and Robert Cecil took his father's place at the head of the Privy Council.

Sir Walter Raleigh, 1554–1618, the Queen's favourite until supplanted by Essex.

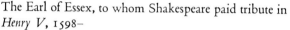

The Earl of Essex, to whom Shakespeare paid tribute in
Henry V, 1598 –

> *Were now the general of our gracious empress,*
> *As in good time he may, from Ireland coming,*
> *Bringing rebellion broached on his sword,*
> *How many would the peaceful city quit*
> *To welcome him!*

His immediate concern was with Ireland, where a nation-wide rebellion had broken out against the English. The Earl of Essex, the Queen's young favourite, was sent to suppress it, but failed ignominiously and was disgraced. Then, as the English helped the Protestants of the Netherlands, so the Spanish helped the Catholics of Ireland, and it was not until the end of the reign that the country was subdued. It was a conquest ruthless as that of England by the Normans, and for once Elizabeth failed tragically to apply her guiding principles of moderation and compromise.

Meanwhile a more glorious revolution had been going on at home: the transformation of the English drama into the greatest of all time. Marlowe died in 1593, but in the last decade of Elizabeth's reign Shakespeare wrote some twenty plays, from *Henry VI* to *Hamlet*, and in 1598 acted in Ben Jonson's first important comedy. Apart from Wyatt, England had produced no major poet since Chaucer, but now came the wonderful flowering: Spenser, Chapman, Daniel, Drayton, Jonson and Donne were all writing at this time, and complementary to them was the new generation of musicians, from Dowland to

This Figure, that thou here seest put,
It was for gentle Shakespeare cut.

The engraving by Martin Droeshout, in the first collected edition of the plays, the Folio of 1623.

'Rare Ben Jonson', 1572–1637.

John Donne, 1573–1631.

John Bull, 1563–1628, first Professor of Music at Gresham College.

Orlando Gibbons, 1583–1625.

Hardwick Hall, Derbyshire, built 1590–97.

The Old East India House in Leadenhall Street.

Orlando Gibbons, who, with Byrd and Morley, made England, for the only time in its history, the leading musical country in Europe. Then in prose there was Hakluyt's *Voyages and Discoveries of the English Nation*, one being James Lancaster's voyage to the East Indies by the Cape route, which led to the foundation of the East India Company in 1600. There was the worldly wisdom of Bacon's *Essays* and Richard Hooker's judicious *Ecclesiastical Polity*, a defence of the Anglican Church and the established order: for 'obedience of creatures unto the law of nature is the stay of the whole world'. Shakespeare had said the same thing time and again.

For an order had been established; not an order imposed by a despot, but one worked out by the Crown and Privy Council in partnership with Parliament. It was an upper- and middle-class disposition, it is true, for the great mass of the people were unrepresented in Parliament, but it was overwhelmingly a contented and prosperous society, united by a Common Law, a common Bible, a Book of Common Prayer, a common language and now a common literature; and Daniel, peering into the future, foresaw a union greater still:

> And who in time knowes whither we may vent
> The treasure of our tongue, to what strange shores
> This gaine of our best glorie shal be sent,
> T'inrich vnknowing Nations with our stores?
> What worlds in th' yet vnformed Occident
> May come refin'd with th' accents that are ours?

Yet the order so carefully nurtured was not altogether secure: there was still a number of unreconciled Catholics, and at the other extreme the Puritans were a repressed but expanding force – and then Elizabeth was nearly seventy, childless, and had not named a successor.

Confusion threatened in 1601 when the sulking Essex tried to raise the Londoners and 'liberate the Queen from her evil counsellors' – ominous words. But Cecil was prepared, and the young earl brought to trial. 'I protest upon my soul,' cried Attorney-General Coke, 'I do believe the Queen should not have long lived after she had been in your power. Note but the precedents of former ages: How long lived Richard II after he was surprised in the same manner? The pretence was alike for the removing of certain counsellors, but yet shortly after it cost him his life.' It was a fearful thought that the anarchy of the fifteenth century might be repeated in the seventeenth. But Essex perished on the block, and when the Queen died in the spring of 1603 Cecil secured a peaceful transition from Tudor to Stuart, and James VI of Scotland became James I of England.

The Coronation of James I and Anne in Westminster Abbey, 25 July 1603. It was a hurried ceremony, as severe plague had just begun in London.

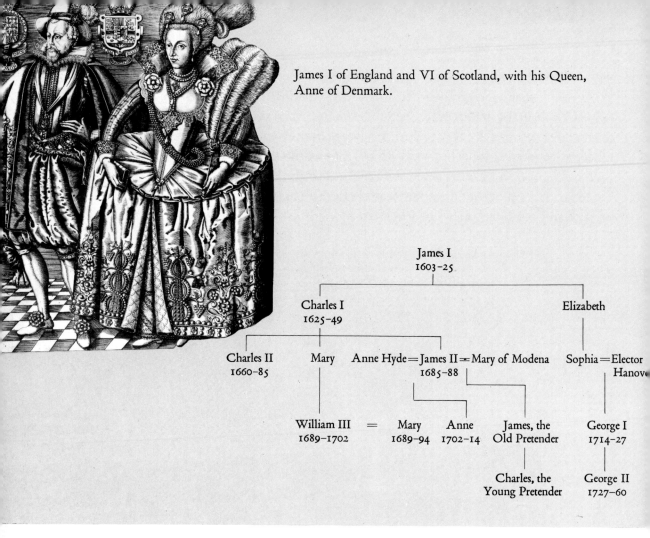

James I of England and VI of Scotland, with his Queen, Anne of Denmark.

James I
1603–25

Charles I
1625–49

Elizabeth

Charles II
1660–85

Mary

Anne Hyde = James II = Mary of Modena
1685–88

Sophia = Elector Hanov[er]

William III
1689–1702

= Mary
1689–94

Anne
1702–14

James, the
Old Pretender

George I
1714–27

Charles, the
Young Pretender

George II
1727–60

8
King, Parliament and Civil War 1603–1649

James I was the first king of the four countries of the British Isles; not of a United Kingdom, however, for though England and Wales had been united by Henry VIII, Scotland and Ireland remained separate realms with their own Parliaments. Nor was England altogether united in its reception of the Scottish king. Raleigh was suspected of plotting against him and imprisoned in the Tower, and in 1605 Guy Fawkes and a group of fanatical Catholics tried to blow up king, ministers and Parliament together. Meanwhile James, who detested the democratic presbyterianism of Scotland, had offended the English Puritans by telling them that if they did not conform to the Anglican Church he would 'harry them out of the land', and three hundred clergy were ejected from their livings.

It was an inauspicious beginning, and Fate could scarcely have sent a more inappropriate monarch than James to rule England at this juncture. A coarse, conceited pedant without any understanding of the English people and their institutions, he presided over a sycophantic Court, the declining standards of which were reflected in the themes of the drama: in the great tragedies of Shakespeare and Webster, the

The execution of Guy Fawkes and other conspirators, opposite the Parliament House, 31 January 1606.

savage satires of Jonson and shallow tragi-comedies of Beaumont and Fletcher. The bright, linear art of the Middle Ages and the Elizabethans gave place to one more sombre and full of shadow.

But at least James was a man of peace, and one of his first acts was to put an end to the twenty years' war with Spain. Unfortunately peace led to neglect of the navy, and the colonization and trade expansion of the reign owed little to government support, a grave disadvantage when the Dutch were setting up trading stations in the East Indies and on the Hudson River in America, and the French establishing themselves on the St Lawrence. Although Sir Humphrey Gilbert had claimed Newfoundland for Elizabeth in 1583, there were no English settlements overseas when the Queen died, and the British Empire began with the foundation of Virginia in 1607, an epoch-making event that was followed by the Puritan emigration of the Pilgrim Fathers who, failing to reach Virginia, settled at Plymouth in what came to be called New England. Barbados and Bermuda were also occupied and, more momentous, the East India Company gained its first foothold in India with the establishment of a trading station at Surat. Less happy was the government's treatment of Ireland as a colony, and the settlement in Ulster of some thousands of Presbyterian Scots, the Catholic Irish being relegated to reserves like the natives of some primitive country.

It was no worse than the Elizabethan conquest, but James had none of the qualities of the great queen. Elizabeth had worked with Parliament, but James maintained that Parliament was there merely to ratify his decisions and grant the money he demanded, for, in his own words, he was 'King by divine hereditary right' and 'God's lieutenant upon earth'. At this time Parliament made no claim to control the administration, which it recognized as the king's province, but it did claim to lay down the general principles by which the king governed; and so began the struggle for self-government and an ordered liberty against an imposed despotic order after the continental model. It was not a struggle for democracy; as the barons at the time of Magna Carta had been concerned only with their own privileges, so Parliament was concerned with the privileges of the upper and middle classes of which

The Indian village of Pomeiooc, Virginia.

it was composed and which it represented – nobility, gentry, lawyers, moneyed merchants – but it was a step towards the liberty of all.

James quarrelled with his first Parliament over his right to levy higher duties on imported goods, and for ten years he managed without it, but by 1621 he had to call another. The Thirty Years' War of religion which involved most of Europe had begun, and one of the Protestant leaders was the German prince who had married James's daughter, Elizabeth. James needed money to help him, but he also thought he might bring about peace by marrying his son Charles to a Spanish princess. Parliament protested against a Catholic alliance, asserting its right to be consulted on all matters of policy, and James angrily dissolved it. Two years later he was drawn into war with Spain, and his reign ended in military disaster.

Yet, despite this miserable and ominous conclusion, it was a reign of astonishing triumphs. It saw the publication of the Authorized Version of the Bible, perhaps the finest prose work in our language, the greatest plays of Shakespeare, from *Othello* to *The Tempest*, the first classical buildings in England, those of Inigo Jones, the beginning of the British Empire and of English science. William Gilbert published his *De Magnete*, the foundation of the science of electricity, just before James's accession; when Shakespeare died in 1616 William Harvey was delivering his epoch-making lectures on the circulation of the blood, and Francis Bacon, like his thirteenth-century namesake, Roger Bacon, was preparing the way for the exact experimental science of the new age. Much, however, of a different nature was to happen in the meantime.

One of the first classical buildings in England: the Banqueting House, Whitehall, designed by Inigo Jones, 1619–22. On the right is the gatehouse, the so-called 'Holbein's Gate', built by Henry VIII, and demolished 1759.

Francis Bacon, 1561–1626.

CHAP. XIII.

1 All giftes, 2. 3 how excellent foeuer, are nothing worth without charitie. 4 The praifes therof, and 13 prelation before hope & faith.

Though I fpeake with the tongues of men & of Angels, and haue not charity I am become as founding braffe oꝛa tinkling cymbal.

2　And though I haue the gift of pꝛophefie, and vnderftand all myfteries and all knowledge : and though I haue all faith, fo that I could remooue mountaines, and haue no charitie, I am nothing.

3　And though I beftowe all my goods to feede the pooꝛe, and though I giue my body to bee burned, and haue not charitie, it pꝛofiteth me nothing.

The Authorized Version, *Corinthians I*, chapter 13.

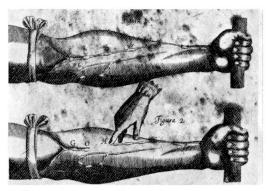

William Harvey, and his experiment demonstrating the circulation of the blood. The pressure of a finger shows that some valves are disposed in one direction, some in another.

Charles I in 1636, after ruling for seven years without Parliament. Van Dyck's triple portrait.

James did not understand the English, but his son Charles I under-stood neither the English nor the Scots. Obstinate as his father but less intelligent, he too believed in his divine hereditary right to rule, though the government was mainly in the hands of his handsome young friend, the Duke of Buckingham, who persuaded him to marry a Catholic French princess, and then dragged England into war with France as well as Spain. Charles himself had Catholic sympathies and naturally favoured the new High Church party of William Laud, soon to be made Archbishop of Canterbury, and as Parliament was becoming increasingly Puritan religious discord was added to political contention.

Events moved quickly in the first four years. Parliament at once attacked the French marriage, Buckingham and the High Church party, and crippled Charles financially by voting him the customary import duties for one year only instead of for life. Charles replied by raising a forced loan and imprisoning those who refused to pay (Magna Carta had stated that 'no freeman shall be imprisoned except by the law of the land'), but further naval and military disasters compelled him to call another Parliament in 1628. Led by Sir John Eliot, John Hampden, John Pym and Sir Edward Coke, defender of the Common Law against prerogative courts like the Star Chamber, they forced the king to accept the Petition of Right: that any tax or loan unauthorized by Parliament was illegal, as was imprisonment of any freeman without cause shown. Buckingham was assassinated while they were demanding his dismissal, but when they attacked Laud, Charles ordered their dissolution. Behind locked doors the Commons passed three resolutions: that anyone who introduced innovations in religion, or advised or paid taxes not granted by Parliament was an enemy of the country. Ignoring the Petition of Right, Charles imprisoned three members, one of them being Eliot, who died in the Tower three years later. Without money, Charles had to withdraw from the war, and while the power of France and Holland grew at the expense of Spain, England lost all authority abroad, and so long as the Crown forced Parliament into opposition there was no hope of recovery.

By reviving old taxes and selling baronetcies, an order created by James I to raise revenue, Charles managed to dispense with Parliament for eleven years, 1629–40. During this period Laud enforced his High Church discipline and so persecuted the Puritans that many of them sought refuge in America, where they founded Massachusetts, Connecticut and other colonies in New England. At the same time, with almost unbelievable stupidity, Charles tried to force the Laudian Church on Presbyterian Scotland. The Scots of course rebelled, and by the summer of 1640 their army had occupied Northumberland and Durham and forced Charles to agree to pay the cost. They knew there was only one way to buy them off, and in November the Long Parliament assembled.

Charles's chief supporter was the brilliant Earl of Strafford, who returned from Ireland where he had been organizing a Catholic army for the king, and the first move of Parliament was to arrest both him and Laud. Then, having passed a series of Acts that limited the power of the crown and reduced it to financial dependence on Parliament, they passed an Act of Attainder against Strafford and made Charles sign the warrant for the execution of his great servant.

Over the political issues Parliament had been unanimous, but when it came to religious matters it began to divide. The Root and Branch Bill abolishing episcopacy, and the Grand Remonstrance demanding a Parliamentary reformation of the Church, were carried only by a small Puritan majority, and when the Militia Bill was introduced transferring the command of army and navy to Parliament Charles, knowing that he had a following in both Houses, tried to arrest Pym, Hampden and other leading members of the Commons, but they escaped to the City of London, where the train-bands rose in their support. A week later Charles fled from Whitehall, and the Commons returned to Westminster. The Civil War had begun.

It was not a selfish and ferocious conflict like the Wars of the Roses, but a war fought mainly for political and religious ideals, splitting society vertically rather than horizontally in classes. Catholics, High Churchmen, most of the Lords and the old gentry were for the king; for Parliament were most of the Puritans and Commons, the industrial areas, the navy, ports, and above all London, wealthiest city in the world. Roughly, the conservative north and west were Royalist, while the more advanced south and east were Parliamentarian. In the short run the king, with his amateur cavalry of hunting squires, had the advantage, but Parliament had the greater staying power, for it had the money to build up a professional disciplined army.

The king's headquarters were at Oxford, and though he failed to take London the first two years of the war were in his favour, largely owing to the exploits of the Cornishmen, who captured Bristol. As a result Parliament made a Solemn League and Covenant with the Scots, in return for whose help they promised to impose Presbyterianism on England. In 1644 this combination of Roundheads, Scots and Cromwell's new cavalry routed the Royalists at Marston Moor, and the north was lost to the king. But the west was saved by the defeat at Lostwithiel of a Parliamentary army that had invaded Cornwall.

Parliament now enlisted a professional New Model Army under the command of Sir Thomas Fairfax and Cromwell, twenty thousand

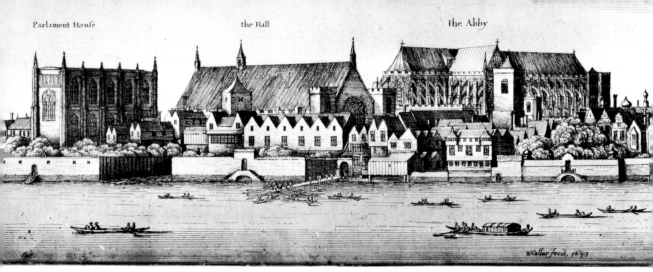

Westminster in 1647, with Parliament House, Westminster Hall and the Abbey.

Two great champions of
Parliament and liberty against
the despotism of Charles I:
John Pym (1584–1643) and
(*right*) Sir John Eliot
(1592–1632).

men many of them 'Independents', opposed both to the established Anglican and Presbyterian Churches, and it was this army that so decisively defeated the Royalists at Naseby and Langport in 1645 that Charles surrendered to the Scots, who handed him over to Parliament.

His policy was now to sow dissension among his opponents, and in this he was helped by the intolerance of Parliament, which attempted to persecute the Independents and disband the Army without pay. Cromwell thereupon seized the king, and offered him generous terms, but his action led to a Second Civil War of the Army against an unnatural alliance of English Presbyterians and Scots with the Royalists. It did not last long: in August 1648 Cromwell defeated his opponents at Preston, and in December he purged Parliament of all its Presbyterians, leaving only a Rump of sixty Independents. The House of Lords was abolished, and the king was tried on a charge of treason against Parliament and the realm. On 30 January 1649 he was executed.

The execution of Charles I in front of the Banqueting House, 30 January 1649.

Apart from any moral considerations, the execution of the king was a tragic blunder, for it roused such a revulsion of feeling that the liberal order for which Cromwell had fought became impossible, and he was compelled to maintain by force the rule of an Independent minority. Even Andrew Marvell in his Ode to Cromwell inserted the lines about Charles:

> He nothing common did or mean
> Upon that memorable scene . . .
>   But bow'd his comely head
>   Down as upon a bed.

Most of the poets of the period, from George Herbert to Henry Vaughan, were Royalists and High Churchmen, and much of their poetry was religious. So was the prose of Sir Thomas Browne, author of the splendid *Religio Medici*, though Milton the Independent wrote a defence of the regicide.

Anarchy threatened. Part of the army mutinied, part of the navy deserted, foreign countries were hostile, Virginia and Barbados withdrew their allegiance, Ireland rebelled, and the Scots proclaimed Charles II, for it was their king whom the English Parliament had killed. Cromwell acted promptly; he imprisoned or shot the mutineers, ruthlessly crushed the Irish, routed the Scots at Dunbar and Worcester, and built a fleet that secured the colonies, wrested Jamaica from Spain, and Admiral Blake defeated the Dutch and made England again mistress of the seas.

Although, except for Catholics and High Churchmen, there was a greater measure of religious toleration than ever before, the government remained a despotism, and when in 1653 Cromwell quarrelled with and expelled the Rump there was nothing but a military dictatorship. All attempts to work with another House of Commons failed, and Cromwell, now Protector of a united Commonwealth of England, Scotland, Ireland and the colonies, was driven to rule by major-generals, each with police powers and an army maintained by taxes on the Royalists.

When Cromwell died in 1658 England fell into the hands of these rival generals, yet it was saved from anarchy by one of them, General Monk, who occupied London and declared for a free Parliament. This Convention Parliament called back Charles II from his long exile in France, and in May 1660 he landed at Dover, a man of thirty, more French than English, amid the joyful acclamations of the people.

The Puritan Republic was a joyless and tragic interlude, yet Cromwell made England a great European power, and simple Englishmen were for the first time allowed free expression of thought without fear of persecution from state or Church, a privilege that was never to be forgotten. A régime that produced George Fox and the Society of Friends was not altogether a failure.

The 'Quakers', an early nickname of the Society of Friends, were constantly persecuted until the Toleration Act of 1689.

Oliver Cromwell, 1599–1658.

The Restoration: the landing of Charles II at Dover. 'The King . . . was received by General Monk with all imaginable love and respect. Infinite the crowd of people. And so into a stately coach there set for him, and so away through the town towards Canterbury.' (*Diary of Samuel Pepys, 23 May 1660.*)

10

From Restoration to Revolution 1660–1688

The Restoration of the Stuarts was the restoration of gaiety, and after being closed for eighteen years the theatres reopened to present the cynical comedies of Wycherley and the new dramatists, written to entertain a corrupt Court determined to enjoy itself after its long exile. It was also the restoration of Parliament, House of Lords, Anglican Church and Cavalier gentry, with all the old abuses of rotten boroughs, intolerance and privilege. But it meant the dissolution of the Common-wealth: although Charles was king of Scotland and Ireland as well as of England, each had its own Parliament again.

Charles himself was an easy-going libertine, clever and un-scrupulous, sceptical, though sympathizing with the Catholicism of his French mother and upbringing, and one of his two main aims was to secure toleration for Catholics. The other was to escape from control of Parliament. But Parliament was determined to retain the control it had gained over Charles I twenty years before: control of taxation, abolition of prerogative courts, and the right to meet at least once every three years. Moreover, no Protestants wanted toleration for Catholics; some favoured toleration for all Protestants, but most of the ruling class wanted to force the whole nation inside the Anglican Church.

For the first seven years Charles left the government to his devoted servant Edward Hyde, Earl of Clarendon, who managed to get an Act of Indemnity and Oblivion passed by the Convention, though he could not prevent the gibbeting of Cromwell's body and execution of a dozen regicides. Then Charles's first Parliament, composed of Cavaliers out for revenge, passed a series of Acts against the Puritans: all who would not conform to the rites of the Anglican Church being deprived of municipal office, expelled from their livings if clergy, imprisoned or transported if they met for religious reasons, and forbidden to come within five miles of a corporate town. These were the years when the Royalists were laughing at the ridicule poured on the Puritans by Samuel Butler in his satirical poem *Hudibras*, but they were also the years when Bunyan was conceiving *The Pilgrim's Progress* and Milton in *Paradise Lost* attempting to 'justify the ways of God to men'.

Young Samuel Pepys of the Navy Office was also writing his diary, among other things recording the events of the Dutch War: the

Edward Hyde, Earl of Clarendon, 1609–74.

John Milton, 1608–74.

Frontispiece portrait and title page of Bunyan's *Pilgrim's Progress*, first published 1678.

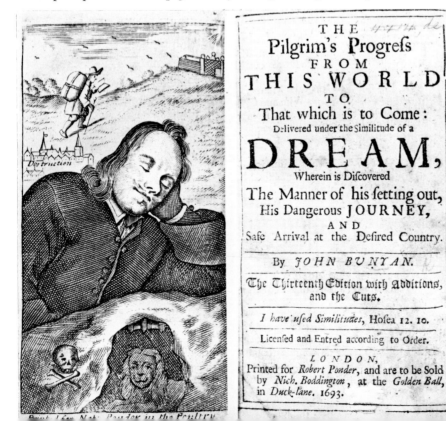

Samuel Pepys, 1633–1703.

123

capture of New Amsterdam, renamed New York after the king's brother, James Duke of York, and, less fortunately, the Great Plague of 1665, the Great Fire of 1666, and the midsummer fire of 1667, when the Dutch sailed up the Thames and burned part of the fleet in the Medway.

These calamities led to the disgrace of Clarendon, and for the next six years Charles governed through an inner Council, or Cabal, of five men, two of whom were Catholics and the other three supporters of religious toleration, the most important being the Earl of Shaftesbury. Having got rid of his Anglican advisers, Charles made the secret Treaty of Dover with Louis XIV of France, who promised him an annual income if he would help him against the Dutch and restore Catholicism in England. This was known only to the Catholic members of the Cabal, and for the benefit of Shaftesbury another treaty was arranged, whereby religious toleration was to be introduced, and England and France were to attack and partition Holland. In 1672, therefore, another Dutch war began, and Charles issued a Declaration of Indulgence granting toleration to all – including Catholics. But he had gone too far: Parliament would have none of it, and Charles had to agree to a Test Act that excluded all Roman Catholics from office under the Crown. To the alarm of the country, one of them proved to be the Duke of York, heir to the throne.

Charles now had to reverse his policy, and for the first time in English history to accept a minister from the party with a majority in Parliament. This was the Earl of Danby, a staunch Anglican, who withdrew from the Dutch war and arranged the marriage of the Duke of York's elder daughter Mary, a Protestant, to Charles's nephew, William of Orange, the heroic defender of Holland against Louis XIV. Danby stood for Church and King, but Shaftesbury was organizing an opposition party composed of those who wanted toleration for Protestants and a Protestant succession. Events played into his hands. In 1678 an unprincipled informer, Titus Oates, swore that he had discovered a Popish plot to murder the king and place the Catholic Duke of York on the throne. Shaftesbury did all he could to inflame opinion; the whole country was soon in a state of panic, and innocent Catholics

A Looking-glasse for City and Countrey:

herein is to be seene many fearfull examples in the time of this grievous Visitation, with an admonition to our Londoners flying from the City; and a perswasion Country to be more pitifull to such as come for succor amongst them.

The 'grievous Visitation' of the Plague in 1665 caused Londoners to flee from the City.

The Great Fire of London, 2–7 September 1666, which destroyed the City including the old Gothic St Paul's Cathedral and eighty-nine churches.

The Earl of Shaftesbury, 1621–83, who tried to secure the succession of the Duke of Monmouth instead of the Catholic James II.

were sent to their deaths on the testimony of Oates. A new Parliament gave Shaftesbury a majority that passed the Habeas Corpus Act, and carried an Exclusion Bill to prevent James's succession. The Lords rejected it, Charles dissolved Parliament, and the country was divided into those who supported and those who opposed exclusion, Whig and Tory being the terms of abuse that they hurled at one another. There was danger of another civil war, but Charles with consummate skill played for time, and by 1681 the Whigs had so discredited them-selves by their violence that Shaftesbury had to fly to Holland, and for the last four years of his reign, despite the Triennial Act, Charles ruled without Parliament. He could afford to do so, for he still drew his allowance from Louis XIV as a reward for his non-interference in Europe, a cynical betrayal of England's safety, for France, not Holland, was the danger.

They were years of Tory triumph and reaction. The persecution of Dissenters was redoubled, leading Whigs were hounded to death, Tory parsons preached a blind devotion to the Stuarts, Tory squires, forgetting their hatred of Catholics in their hatred of Dissenters and Whigs, adulated Charles and James, town charters were revised to produce a Parliament without Whig members, and Dryden published his *Absalom and Achitophel* satirizing Shaftesbury and the Duke of Monmouth, an illegitimate son of Charles, and Shaftesbury's candidate for the succession. At the same time James was conducting an even more atrocious persecution of the Scottish Presbyterians, and Louis driving French Protestants to the Mass or the galleys and pushing his armies into Flanders, opposite England.

To such a pass had religious differences, exploited for political ends, brought Europe, though in England there was one hopeful sign of a more rational age. In 1662 the Royal Society for Improving Natural Knowledge had been incorporated, among its first members being Robert Boyle, John Evelyn, Christopher Wren, Professor of Astronomy at Oxford, and Isaac Newton, Professor of Mathematics at Cambridge. The age of co-operative experimental science had begun, and the victory of knowledge over superstition and fear must be followed by understanding and tolerance. There was, however, a final scene to be played.

When James II succeeded his brother in 1685 he was greeted by a Parliament packed with Tories, but the exiled Whigs were at work, and in June Monmouth landed at Lyme Regis. It was a forlorn rebellion; the western peasants were routed at Sedgemoor, the last battle fought in England, Monmouth was executed, and after the Bloody Assize of Judge Jeffreys three hundred rebels were left hanging beside the roads. Tories as well as Whigs were revolted by this cruelty, but James, feeling secure with an army of thirty thousand men, went on to defy both Tory Parliament and Tory Church. He introduced Catholics into the army and universities, set up a Church Court under Jeffreys, and in 1688 issued and ordered to be read in churches a Declaration of Indulgence that gave toleration to Catholics as well as Dissenters. Most of the clergy refused, and seven bishops were sent to London for

Execution of the Duke of Monmouth, July 1685, on a playing card of the period.

The signature of Charles II as founder of the Royal Society, 1662. His brother James was a Fellow.

The Seven Bishops committed for trial in 1688. 'My Lord of Bristol was the most saucy of the Seven,' said James II. This was Jonathan Trelawny (*lower right*), hero of the song, 'And shall Trelawny die?'

William III lands at Brixham, November 1688.

trial, but were acquitted, to the joy of the whole country. Meanwhile James's Catholic queen had given birth to a son, a Catholic succession seemed assured, and a number of leading Whigs and Tories asked William of Orange to come to the help of England.

William landed at Brixham in November; James's army melted away, and before Christmas he and his baby son had fled to the Court of Louis XIV.

This, just halfway between Armada year and the fall of the Bastille, was the so-called Bloodless Revolution of 1688. The previous decade had been bloody enough, yet there was much to show on the credit side. The Restoration period was one of English expansion, and by 1688 an unbroken chain of self-governing colonies stretched down the American coast from New England to Carolina. To the north of the French settlements in Canada the Hudson Bay Company had been established, and the East India Company, besides its trading stations at Surat, Madras and Calcutta, had acquired its first Indian

Sir Christopher Wren, 1632–1723, and the new London, rebuilt after the Great Fire,

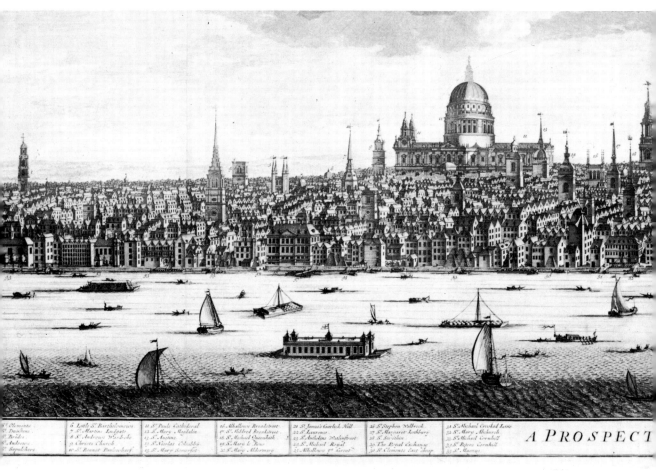

4 Clements	6 Little St Bartholomews	11 St Pauls Cathedral	16 Alhallows Breadstreet	21 St James's Garlick Hill	26 St Stephen Walbrook	31 St Michael Crooked Lane	A PROSPECT
St Dunstans	7 St Martins Ludgate	12 St Mary Magdalen	17 St Mildred Breadstreet	22 St Laurence	27 St Margaret Lothbury	32 St Mary Abchurch	
St Brides	8 St Andrews Wardrobe	13 St Antonin	18 St Michael Queenhith	23 St Antholine Watlingstreet	28 St Swithin	33 St Michael Cornhill	
St Andrews	9 Christs Church	14 St Nicolas Coleabby	19 St Mary le Bow	24 St Michael Royal	29 The Royal Exchange	34 St Peters Cornhill	
St Sepulchres	10 St Bennet Paulswharf	15 St Mary Somerset	20 St Mary Aldermary	25 Alhallows yᵉ Great	30 St Clements East Cheap	35 St Magnus	

territory, Bombay. In England, too, the frontiers were advancing: Wren was rebuilding St Paul's and the City churches, adding new graces to the colleges of Oxford and Cambridge, and, recommended by Evelyn, Grinling Gibbons was adorning their interiors with his wood carving; Purcell in music and Dryden in verse were celebrating St Cecilia; Newton was dedicating his *Principia* to the Royal Society, and Locke writing his *Essay Concerning the Human Understanding*. If it was true that man does not know the 'real essence' of anything, the age of tolerance could not be far off.

with Wren's St Paul's and churches.

CITY of LONDON.

The 'bloodless' and 'glorious' Revolution was also a moderate one; Protestant Stuart had succeeded Catholic; James II had been replaced by his nephew and daughter, William and Mary. The Revolution Settlement was equally moderate. The Bill of Rights was mainly a restatement of what the Crown might not do, and the executive power remained with the King. The Toleration Act gave religious liberty to Protestant non-conformists, though not religious equality; Dissenters as well as Catholics were still excluded from public office and the universities. Yet it was a great step forward; it was Parliament, Tories as well as Whigs, not divine hereditary right, that determined the succession; Parliament was recognized as the supreme law-making body with the power of the purse, a partner with the Crown; and the recognition of the right of the individual conscience was one of the great victories of history.

It was a dangerous Revolution, however, for England had a population of only five million, while France, now at the height of her power, had twenty, and for Louis XIV the King of England was still James II. Fortunately Scotland accepted William and Mary, though the wild highlanders under Viscount Dundee rose for James, only to be defeated at Killiecrankie, and the Macdonalds of Glencoe were treacherously massacred for their delay in taking the oath to William. The Presbyterian system was restored, the Scottish Parliament became fully independent, and only the Crown linked the two countries.

The immediate danger was Ireland, where the Catholics declared for James, who landed with French troops in 1689, and besieged the Protestant stronghold of Londonderry. The siege was raised, but the situation was critical, and when on the banks of the river Boyne in July 1690 an English and Dutch army under William met an Irish and French army under James the fates of England and Europe, as well as Ireland, were in the balance. William's victory saved the English Revolution, and Europe from French domination. But Ireland lost all. Her Parliament was reduced to impotence and, to the shame of England, her Catholics were deprived of almost every human right, including the elementary right to be educated. Although the colonies shared the benefits of the Revolution, Ireland remained an outcast among nations.

The Battle of the Boyne, 1 July 1690, which secured the position of William III and the Revolution Settlement.

William cared nothing for Ireland – or for England, except as a means of saving Holland from Louis XIV, and by 1689 his new king-dom was at war with France. It was in the main a static war of sieges in the Spanish Netherlands, modern Belgium, remarkable only for the great naval victory of La Hogue, which freed England from threat of

The Battle of La Hogue, May 1692, which destroyed Louis XIV's attempt to invade England.

invasion and gave her command of the seas, as the defeat of the Armada had done a century before. The peace made in 1697 was inconclusive, but there were two important consequences of the war. One was the foundation of the Bank of England and the financing of the struggle by loans that formed a permanent National Debt. As this was mainly the work of the wealthy Whigs of the City, it gave them a vested interest in the Revolution Settlement, for a Jacobite restoration would mean the loss of their money. Then, William found that the most efficient government in prosecuting the war was one of men of the same party, an arrangement that was soon to lead to the Cabinet system.

The eighteenth century opened with events that made the renewal of war inevitable. In 1700 Louis's grandson inherited the throne of Spain, which meant French control of the Spanish empire, not only of its possessions in the New World but also of the Netherlands. Then, on the death of James II in 1701, Louis recognized his young son as James III of England. William III died at the beginning of 1702, and as Queen Mary was already dead he was succeeded by Mary's sister Anne. As commander of the army he was succeeded by John Churchill, Duke of Marlborough, most brilliant of all English soldiers, and it was he who, supported at home by his friend, Lord Treasurer Godolphin, destroyed the power of Louis XIV in the War of the Spanish Succession, fought to place an Austrian instead of a French prince on the throne of Spain.

Marlborough had no intention of being tied down to another war of sieges in the Netherlands, and in 1704 marched rapidly up the Rhine to the Danube, where he joined the Austrians, and at Blenheim utterly routed the combined French and Bavarian army. It was a staggering blow for Louis, the beginning of the rapid decline of his power, and to add to his discomfiture, a few days before Blenheim an English fleet took Gibraltar. All England rejoiced except the Tory politicians, and the Queen gave Marlborough the royal manor of Woodstock on which she commissioned Vanbrugh to build Blenheim Palace at her expense.

Two years later Marlborough's great victory at Ramillies drove the French out of the Netherlands, while his Austrian ally drove them out

The capture of Gibraltar, July 1704.

Marlborough's victory at Blenheim, 13 August 1704.

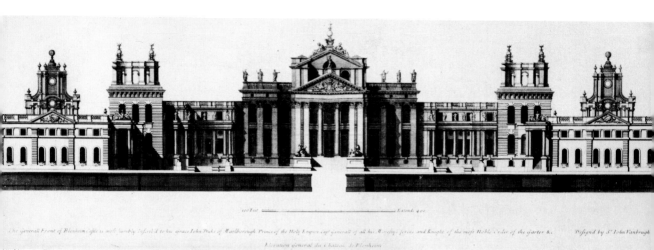

Blenheim Palace

'See, Sir, here's the grand approach,
This way is for his Grace's coach . . .
The council chamber's for debate,
And all the rest are rooms of state.'
'Thanks, Sir,' I cried, '' tis very fine,
But where d'ye sleep and where d'ye dine?
I find by all you have been telling,
That 'tis a house but not a dwelling.'

(Pope)

John Churchill,
1st Duke of Marlborough, 1650–1722.

of Italy, and Louis sued for peace. But the Whigs were so elated by their successes that instead of negotiating a treaty with the French they negotiated an Act of Union with the Scots. In May 1707 the two Parliaments were united and the island became Great Britain with its symbolic flag, the Union Jack. Although the Scots retained their Presbyterian Church and their own legal system, the Union was not immediately popular, but the two countries were soon to find the immense political and economic advantages of co-operation. It was the creation of order on a new scale.

Meanwhile the war was vigorously prosecuted; in 1708 a British fleet seized Minorca, and by routing the French at Oudenarde Marlborough opened the way for an advance into France. Again Louis asked for peace, but Marlborough pressed on, and in Canada Nova Scotia was wrested from the French. But the Whig government was tottering: the Tories had a majority in the Commons, and they had never been wholeheartedly in favour of a war that made money for the Whigs. Then the Queen, having quarrelled with her old friend the Duchess of Marlborough, fell under the influence of the Tory leader Harley, and in 1710 dismissed Godolphin and his ministry. Marlborough was recalled, and in 1713 the Tories made the Treaty of Utrecht. Austria was to have the Spanish Netherlands, the crowns of France and Spain were never to be united, and Britain retained Gibraltar, Minorca, Nova Scotia and Newfoundland. It was a moderate peace after a war that was prologue to two centuries of British ascendancy.

England, however, was divided. The High Church Tories were in power, by various measures trying to destroy the Whig party and weaken the Dissenters, while the extremists, led by the Earl of Bolingbroke, were planning a Jacobite restoration, although the Act of Settlement assigned the crown to James I's Protestant descendants of the House of Hanover if Anne died childless. All Anne's children were dead: by July 1714 she herself was dying, and before Bolingbroke could mature his plans she was dead.

It was a brief but triumphant reign, celebrated in the grandiose baroque edifices of Vanbrugh and paintings of Sir James Thornhill,

Ceiling of the Painted Hall at
Greenwich, by Sir James Thornhill,
c. 1710. A fine example of the grand
manner of the period, representing 'The
Landing of William III' and 'The
Landing of George I', 'as they should
have been, rather than as they were'.

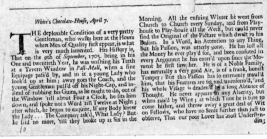

The first number of *The Tatler*, 12 April 1709.

Isaac Newton, 1642–1727.

John Dryden, 1631–1700.

Jonathan Swift, 1667–1745.

in the florid music of Handel, opera, organ and oratorio, strange contrasts to the lucid and restrained writing of the period:

> 'Tis more to guide than spur the Muse's steed,
> Restrain his fury than provoke his speed,

wrote Pope, introducing the age of reason, classical balance and moderation. It was primarily an age of prose: Congreve's great comedy *The Way of the World* was produced in 1700, Swift published *The Tale of a Tub* satirizing both Roman Catholics and extreme Protestants in the year of Blenheim, and the last years of Anne were those of the *Spectator*, the periodical for which Steele and Addison wrote their essays, notably those about the Tory squire, Sir Roger de Coverley.

139

Soon after Queen Anne's death Hanoverian George arrived in London. In the last seven hundred years England had had Danish, Norman, French, Welsh, Scottish and Dutch sovereigns, and now the Whigs had brought over an elderly and unprepossessing German who could speak no English. This had momentous consequences, for George I handed over to his Whig protectors many of the royal prerogatives and left the chairmanship of his Council to their leader, who thus became president of an executive committee of the party with a majority in the Commons; in other words, a Prime Minister presiding over a Cabinet, the members of which had to agree on all major points of policy.

Although most of the local squires were Tories, the party had destroyed itself as an alternative government by its excesses, and the great Whig families, whose heads sat in the Lords, controlled the Commons. This was easy enough when the royal patronage, which meant bribery as well as preferment, was in their hands, when the electorate was so small, and landlords knew for whom their tenants voted, for there was no secret ballot. In this way the Whig oligarchy perpetuated its power for half a century, yet, though it was purely selfish in its aims, it brought peace, toleration and prosperity after the long years of strife and persecution. A spirit of moderation and common-sense pervaded the Whig Church, universities and the arts, in all of which enthusiasm and excess were deplored, and in spite of gross inequalities, indifference and brutality, the people of England, still predominantly villagers, were probably more contented than ever before.

There was, therefore, little English support for the half-hearted Jacobite rising of 1715 on behalf of James II's son, the Old Pretender; people were more interested in gambling in trade with the tropics, particularly in the stock of the South Sea Company, and it was the bursting of this speculative bubble, involving widespread ruin, that brought Sir Robert Walpole into power in 1721 to clean up the mess. For twenty-one years he managed the Whig machine, preserving peace and developing the Cabinet system, and, though he would have deprecated the title as savouring too much of continental despotism, he was really the first Prime Minister.

Alexander Pope, 1688–1744.

His policy was 'to let sleeping dogs lie', and for the two decades of his ministry little occurred to upset the tranquillity of the country, the accession of George II in 1727 making no difference to the dependence of the Crown on the Whigs. It was the age of Pope, *Gulliver's Travels* and *Robinson Crusoe* (another South Sea inspiration), of Handel, Hogarth and Gay's *Beggar's Opera*, partly a satire directed against Walpole and political corruption. Some of the scenes take place in prison, and it was against the horrors of the debtors' prisons that General Oglethorpe protested, and in 1733 founded the colony of Georgia as a refuge for the poor and distressed. John Wesley went there three years later, and after his return began his great life-work of evangelism, fifty years of preaching to those whom the somnolent Church neglected.

That was in 1739, the year in which Walpole was forced against his will into a maritime war with Spain, which soon involved a continental war in defence of Austria against France and most of the continental powers. As a result Walpole fell, for he was no war minister, his place being taken for the next twenty years by Henry Pelham and his brother the Duke of Newcastle, who was even more

The first Prime Minister, Sir Robert
Walpole, Whig Prime Minister 1721–42,
talking to the Speaker, Sir Richard
Onslow, in the House of Commons.

The South Sea Bubble and general 'share
madness' of the time is satirized
in this print of 1720. Even 'A Company
for carrying on an Undertaking of great
Advantage, but nobody to know what it is,'
had a thousand subscribers.

A scene from Gay's *Beggar's Opera* (1728) painted by Hogarth.

'Robinson Crusoe' was another South Sea
inspiration. This woodcut is from
a 1753 edition.

John Wesley, 1703–91, founder of Methodism.
'To promote vital practical religion' he travelled some
5,000 miles a year and preached two sermons a day.

Final defeat of the Jacobite cause at Culloden, 16 April 1746.

shamelessly corrupt in his management of the Whig party. The war lasted eight years, and settled nothing, though it offered a golden opportunity for another Jacobite rebellion while the British army was engaged in Flanders.

In 1745, encouraged by the promise of French help, the Young Pretender, Charles Edward, landed with seven followers on the west coast of Scotland. The Highlanders rose in support of the romantic young man, occupied Edinburgh, scattered a small British force at Prestonpans, and by the beginning of December reached Derby. But the northern English Jacobites did not join him, there was no help from France, British troops from Flanders had returned, and the long retreat began. The end came on Culloden Moor near Inverness, where the Highlanders were routed. There followed a cruel harrying of the glens, the feudal clan loyalties were abolished, and the wild Highlanders at last brought under the control of the central government. Charles Edward escaped, but it was the last attempt to restore the Stuarts.

Culloden was the year in which the Venetian painter Canaletto, distressed by the lack of English patrons during the war, came to England to paint his pictures of Georgian London and the new City raised by Wren from the ashes of the old. It would have been worth his travelling to Bath, which the Woods, father and son, were transforming into the most beautiful town in England, worthy of the elegant manners that Beau Nash was teaching its fashionable visitors. They

London Bridge from the south-west, c. 1750, by Canaletto.

The Circus at Bath, designed by John Wood and begun 1754.

William Pitt,
1st Earl of Chatham,
organizer of victory,
1708–78.

were the eager readers of the first real novels in our language, *Tom Jones* and the other works of Fielding, and the picaresque romances of Smollet all appearing between the publication of Richardson's *Pamela* in 1740 and Sterne's *Tristram Shandy* in 1760. More controversial was the scepticism of David Hume's *Philosophical Essays*.

The war, which ended in 1748, was followed by a few uneasy years of peace, and while the melancholy lines of Gray's *Elegy* were becoming almost a part of men's lives, England and France were jockeying for position at opposite ends of the earth. The great Mogul Empire in India was breaking up into innumerable independent states, with the rulers of which the English and French East India Companies were making rival alliances. In America the French government, by erecting forts along the rivers St Lawrence, upper Hudson, Ohio and Mississippi, were confining to the coast the thirteen British colonies, too jealous of one another to act in concert. By 1755 there was fighting on the Hudson, and in 1756 the struggle became part of another great European conflict, the Seven Years' War of England and Prussia against France and Austria.

The first years were disastrous: in America a British force was cut to pieces; in India the traders of Calcutta suffered the horror of the Black Hole; Frederick the Great of Prussia was surrounded by enemies; Minorca was lost and Admiral Byng shot 'pour encourager les autres'. Newcastle and the others needed encouragement, but this was given in full measure when William Pitt joined the ministry, and with an incomparable grasp of world strategy and complete confidence in himself, began to organize the conduct of the war.

The first thing was to contain the French in Europe by blockading their naval ports, by subsidizing Frederick and sending troops to Hanover to help him. 'I will conquer Canada in Germany,' Pitt said, and the inability of the French to send reinforcements to America was their undoing. One by one their fortresses fell to a pincer movement from east and west: Louisburg at the mouth of the St Lawrence, Fort Duquesne (renamed Pittsburgh) on the Ohio, Oswego and Frontenac on Lake Ontario. Then in 1759 came the Year of Victories: the naval victories of Lagos and Quiberon Bay, of Minden in Hanover and, to

The Year of Victories – General James Wolfe captures Quebec, the key to Canada, 13 September 1759.

crown all, Wolfe's capture of the central French citadel of Quebec. Meanwhile Frederick had won two great battles, and Clive's victory at Plassey and the final defeat of the French near Madras gave the East India Company complete control over the native rulers of the huge provinces of Bengal and the Carnatic.

By the Peace of Paris in 1763 France ceded all Canada to Britain and all her territory west of the thirteen colonies, while in India the French were reduced to two small trading stations. It was a tremendous acquisition of empire.

The peace was not made by Pitt, however. In 1760 George II was succeeded by his grandson George III, a young man who 'gloried in the name of Briton' and saw himself as the hero of Bolingbroke's *Patriot King*: a king who really ruled and chose whom he liked as his ministers. He resumed the royal patronage, therefore, and the Whig oligarchy, deprived of the means that had kept them in power for nearly half a century, collapsed. It was back to 1689: the end, or rather suspension, of Cabinet government, and the beginning of a disastrous period of rule by the King and the 'King's Friends'.

George spent the first ten years of his reign trying to find the right men as his servants. Pitt, though himself a non-party man, went in 1761, and as ministry followed ministry relations with the American colonies deteriorated. They were not without grievance: although, unlike the colonies of any other country, they were self-governing, Britain regulated their trade in her own interests, and now insisted that they should help to pay for the highly expensive war in their defence. This was not unreasonable, but as the colonies, disunited and jealous of one another, would not tax themselves, the Parliament at Westminister prepared to do the taxing. Not unreasonably the colonists protested, and now that the French menace had been removed they were in a stronger position to protest. 'No taxation without representation' became their watch-word. Edward I had said the same thing five hundred years before: 'What touches all should be approved by all.' But Parliament imposed a stamp duty on legal documents, repealed it, imposed duties on various imports and, after riots in Boston, repealed all save a tax on tea.

The Parliament that was thus alienating the colonists was the one that made a hero of the scurrilous John Wilkes by expelling him from the Commons and then, when he was returned as member for Middlesex, declaring his opponent elected. To such a pass had the Patriot King, with the Commons in his pocket, brought parliamentary government.

In the spring of 1770, when Captain Cook was hoisting the Union Jack at Botany Bay on the newly discovered east coast of Australia, the king found the perfectly obsequious servant in Lord North, one who would manage his Parliament while he mismanaged affairs. The

The Patriot King.

The Birth of a Nation – Britain's thirteen American colonies declare their independence, 4 July 1776.

IN CONGRESS, JULY 4, 1776.

The unanimous Declaration of the thirteen united States of America.

When in the Course of human events it becomes necessary for one people to dissolve the political bands which have connected them with another, and to assume among the powers of the earth, the separate and equal station to which the Laws of Nature and of Nature's God entitle them, a decent respect to the opinions of mankind requires that they should declare the causes which impel them to the separation. — We hold these truths to be self-evident, that all men are created equal, that they are endowed by their Creator with certain unalienable Rights, that among these are Life, Liberty and the pursuit of Happiness — That to secure these rights, Governments are instituted among Men, deriving their just powers from the consent of the governed, — That whenever any Form of Government becomes destructive of these ends, it is the Right of the People to alter or to abolish it, and to institute new Government, laying its foundation on such principles and organizing its powers in such form, as to them shall seem most likely to effect their Safety and Happiness. Prudence, indeed, will dictate that Governments long established should not be changed for light and transient causes; and accordingly all experience hath shewn, that mankind are more disposed to suffer, while evils are sufferable, than to right themselves by abolishing the forms to which they are accustomed. But when a long train of abuses and usurpations, pursuing invariably the same Object evinces a design to reduce them under absolute Despotism, it is their right, it is their duty, to throw off such Government, and to provide new Guards for their future security. — Such has been the patient sufferance of these Colonies; and such is now the necessity which constrains them to alter their former Systems of Government. The history of the present King of Great Britain is a history of repeated injuries and usurpations, all having in direct object the establishment of an absolute Tyranny over these States. To prove this, let Facts be submitted to a candid world.

He has refused his Assent to Laws, the most wholesome and necessary for the public good. — He has forbidden his Governors to pass Laws of immediate and pressing importance, unless suspended in their operation till his Assent should be obtained; and when so suspended, he has utterly neglected to attend to them. — He has refused to pass other Laws for the accommodation of large districts of people, unless those people would relinquish the right of Representation in the Legislature, a right inestimable to them and formidable to tyrants only. — He has called together legislative bodies at places unusual, uncomfortable, and distant from the depository of their public Records, for the sole purpose of fatiguing them into compliance with his measures. — He has dissolved Representative Houses repeatedly, for opposing with manly firmness his invasions on the rights of the people. — He has refused for a long time, after such dissolutions, to cause others to be elected; whereby the Legislative powers, incapable of Annihilation, have returned to the People at large for their exercise; the State remaining in the mean time exposed to all the dangers of invasion from without, and convulsions within. — He has endeavoured to prevent the population of these States; for that purpose obstructing the Laws for Naturalization of Foreigners; refusing to pass others to encourage their migrations hither, and raising the conditions of new Appropriations of Lands. — He has obstructed the Administration of Justice, by refusing his Assent to Laws for establishing Judiciary powers. — He has made Judges dependent on his Will alone, for the tenure of their offices, and the amount and payment of their salaries. — He has erected a multitude of New Offices, and sent hither swarms of Officers to harrass our people, and eat out their substance. — He has kept among us, in times of peace, Standing Armies without the Consent of our legislatures. — He has affected to render the Military independent of and superior to the Civil power. — He has combined with others to subject us to a jurisdiction foreign to our constitution, and unacknowledged by our laws; giving his Assent to their Acts of pretended Legislation: — For quartering large bodies of armed troops among us: — For protecting them, by a mock Trial, from punishment for any Murders which they should commit on the Inhabitants of these States: — For cutting off our Trade with all parts of the world: — For imposing Taxes on us without our Consent: — For depriving us in many cases, of the benefits of Trial by jury: — For transporting us beyond Seas to be tried for pretended offences — For abolishing the free System of English Laws in a neighbouring Province, establishing therein an Arbitrary government, and enlarging its Boundaries so as to render it at once an example and fit instrument for introducing the same absolute rule into these Colonies: — For taking away our Charters, abolishing our most valuable Laws, and altering fundamentally the Forms of our Governments: — For suspending our own Legislatures, and declaring themselves invested with power to legislate for us in all cases whatsoever. — He has abdicated Government here, by declaring us out of his Protection and waging War against us. — He has plundered our seas, ravaged our Coasts, burnt our towns, and destroyed the lives of our people. — He is at this time transporting large Armies of foreign Mercenaries to compleat the works of death, desolation and tyranny, already begun with circumstances of Cruelty & perfidy scarcely paralleled in the most barbarous ages, and totally unworthy the Head of a civilized nation. — He has constrained our fellow Citizens taken Captive on the high Seas to bear Arms against their Country, to become the executioners of their friends and Brethren, or to fall themselves by their Hands. — He has excited domestic insurrections amongst us, and has endeavoured to bring on the inhabitants of our frontiers, the merciless Indian Savages, whose known rule of warfare, is an undistinguished destruction of all ages, sexes and conditions. — In every stage of these Oppressions We have Petitioned for Redress in the most humble terms: Our repeated Petitions have been answered only by repeated injury. A Prince whose character is thus marked by every act which may define a Tyrant, is unfit to be the ruler of a free people. Nor have We been wanting in attentions to our British brethren. We have warned them from time to time of attempts by their legislature to extend an unwarrantable jurisdiction over us. We have reminded them of the circumstances of our emigration and settlement here. We have appealed to their native justice and magnanimity, and we have conjured them by the ties of our common kindred to disavow these usurpations, which, would inevitably interrupt our connections and correspondence. They too have been deaf to the voice of justice and of consanguinity. We must, therefore, acquiesce in the necessity, which denounces our Separation, and hold them, as we hold the rest of mankind, Enemies in War, in Peace Friends. —

We, therefore, the Representatives of the united States of America, in General Congress, Assembled, appealing to the Supreme Judge of the world for the rectitude of our intentions, do, in the Name, and by Authority of the good People of these Colonies, solemnly publish and declare, That these United Colonies are, and of Right ought to be Free and Independent States; that they are Absolved from all Allegiance to the British Crown, and that all political connection between them and the State of Great Britain, is and ought to be totally dissolved; and that as Free and Independent States, they have full Power to levy War, conclude Peace, contract Alliances, establish Commerce, and to do all other Acts and Things which Independent States may of right do. — And for the support of this Declaration, with a firm reliance on the Protection of divine Providence, we mutually pledge to each other our Lives, our Fortunes and our sacred Honor.

John Hancock

Button Gwinnett
Lyman Hall
Geo Walton.

Wm Hooper
Joseph Hewes,
John Penn

Edward Rutledge.

Thos Heyward Junr.
Thomas Lynch Junr.
Arthur Middleton

Samuel Chase
Wm Paca
Thos Stone
Charles Carroll of Carrollton

George Wythe
Richard Henry Lee
Th Jefferson
Benja Harrison
Thos Nelson jr.
Francis Lightfoot Lee
Carter Braxton

Robt Morris
Benjamin Rush
Benja Franklin
John Morton
Geo Clymer
Jas Smith.
Geo Taylor
James Wilson
Geo Ross
Caesar Rodney
Geo Read
Tho M:Kean

Wm Floyd
Phil. Livingston
Frans Lewis
Lewis Morris

Richd Stockton
Jno Witherspoon
Fras Hopkinson
John Hart
Abra Clark

Josiah Bartlett
Wm Whipple
Saml Adams
John Adams
Robt Treat Paine
Elbridge Gerry
Step Hopkins
William Ellery
Roger Sherman
Saml Huntington
Wm Williams
Oliver Wolcott
Matthew Thornton

result was the Boston Tea Party of 1773, when the colonists threw the East India Company's tea into the harbour. Parliament replied by passing penal measures against Massachusetts and cancelling its charter. Pitt, now Earl of Chatham, vehemently opposed this disastrous policy, as did Edmund Burke and his young friend Charles Fox, leaders of a regenerated Whig party; but it was too late. In the early summer of 1775 there were skirmishes at Lexington and Bunker's Hill near Boston, and in June the Congress of the United Colonies at Philadelphia elected George Washington of Virginia commander of their armed forces. A year later, 4 July 1776, Congress issued a Declaration of Independence, a few months after Gibbon had published the first volume of his *Decline and Fall of the Roman Empire*.

Fortunately for Britain, Canada remained loyal, and as there were many Loyalists in the middle colonies, the British occupied New York with the object of driving a wedge between New England and the southern states along the line of the Hudson; but General Burgoyne, advancing south from Montreal in 1777, was surrounded at Saratoga and compelled to surrender.

It was the turning-point of the war. Encouraged by the defeat of their old adversary, the despotic powers of France and Spain proclaimed themselves champions of American liberty and declared war on Britain. In 1780 they were joined by Holland, and most of the other European powers formed a hostile League of Armed Neutrality. At the same time Protestants and Catholics in Ireland combined under Henry Grattan to force the government to free their Parliament and trade from British control, and for four days at the beginning of 1780 London was in the hands of an anti-Catholic mob led by the crazy Lord George Gordon. No wonder the Commons carried a motion that 'the influence of the Crown has increased, is increasing, and ought to be diminished'.

Botany Bay in the eighteenth century.

Captain Cook, 1728–79.

Chatham was dead, and Britain, directed by the King and North, was confronted by the western world in arms; but she was saved by a few great men: Warren Hastings saved India, Sir Guy Carleton kept Canada loyal, Sir George Elliott held Gibraltar, and for most of the time Admiral Rodney managed to keep command of the seas. For a few fatal weeks, however, he lost it, and in October 1781 a British force in Yorktown on the Virginian coast was caught between a Franco-American army and a French fleet and forced to surrender.

The war was virtually over, and when peace was made in 1782 Britain ceded all her territory south of Canada to the thirteen colonies, which set about transforming themselves into the United States of America with Washington as their President.

The first British empire had fallen, and with it ended the fatal period of George III's personal government, the last attempt of the Crown to direct the affairs of Britain. Lord North resigned and the Cabinet system was restored, with a Prime Minister who was head of the party with a majority in the Commons, to which he was responsible. It was not a restoration of the old Whig oligarchy, however, for the new Whigs carried Burke's Economic Reform Bill, which made it impossible for a government to buy a majority in Parliament. But George preferred the new Tories to the new Whigs, and in 1783 invited William Pitt the younger, Chatham's twenty-four year old son, to form a ministry.

The period of George III's personal rule was precisely that of young Boswell's friendship with the literary dictator of the age, Dr Johnson. They met in 1763, the year before the formation of the Literary Club, among whose members were Sir Joshua Reynolds, Goldsmith, Burke, Fox, Garrick, Gibbon, Sheridan and Adam Smith. Reynolds, Gainsborough and Richard Wilson were all at the height of their

Charles James Fox, 1749–1806.   Adam Smith, 1723–90.   David Garrick, 1717–79.   Edmund Burke, 1729–97.

powers as painters, and Robert Adam was transforming the interiors of the great houses of the nobility. It was the climax of the classical age in England, an elegant age that seemed to be so firmly established that there was no reason why it should ever end. Yet it may be said to have ended in 1784 with the advent of Pitt and death of Johnson, who left the world to the revolutionary thinkers whom he so much distrusted: to scientists like Joseph Priestley, the discoverer of oxygen, to economists like Adam Smith, whose *Wealth of Nations* appeared in the year of the Declaration of Independence, and engineers like James Watt, who in 1782 succeeded in harnessing machinery to the steam engine.

Pitt, Speaker Onslow, Johnson, Garrick
and other celebrities at Tunbridge Wells in 1748.

1748 1 Aug: 3   4   5   6   7   8   9   10 11 12 13 14   15 16   17   18 19 20   21

Dr. Johnson   6 Mrs. Trase   11 Ld. Powis   16 The Baron
Bp. of Salisbury   7 Mr. Nash   12 Dutches of Norfolk   17 Anonym
Ld. Harcourt   8 Miss Chudleigh   13 Miss Banks   18 Mrs. Onslow
Mr. Cibber   9 Mr. Pitt   14 Lady Lincoln   19 Miss Onslow
Mr. Garrick   10 A. O. Esqr   15 Mr. Lyttelton   20 Mrs. Johnson
                                                                         21 Mr. W...

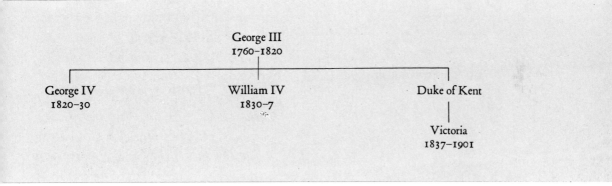

Book Three

George III
1760–1820

George IV
1820–30

William IV
1830–7

Duke of Kent

Victoria
1837–1901

The England of 1784, when Johnson died, was not so very different from the England of his youth. There were more people, of course, some seven million perhaps instead of six, but their way of life had not greatly altered. There were no big manufacturing towns, and the unit was still the village, where crafts were practised in the home, women spinning and men weaving on their hand looms. Most families, therefore, owned some means of making a living: land, or the right of common pasture, or simple wooden machines. In the ports ships were much the same as those of Pepys's day, and even the art of poetry was a perpetuation of the couplets of Dryden and Pope. Coal, where available, was for domestic use, almost the only sources of power, apart from a primitive steam pump, being wind and water, and men knew little more about the laws of nature than Newton had taught them.

14
*The Industrial
Revolution
and
Napoleonic
War
1783–1830*

153

Richard Arkwright's Water Frame, 1769, which revolutionized cotton spinning.

There had been some agricultural improvement in the middle years of the century, and some conversion of medieval open fields into consolidated holdings where better farming could be practised; but improvement became revolution in the 1780s when Thomas Coke of Norfolk began the scientific farming of his Holkham estates, raising their annual value tenfold, and Arthur Young, from 1784 onwards, disseminated the new techniques in his *Annals of Agriculture*. The Midlands, scarcely affected by Tudor enclosure for sheep pasture, were rapidly enclosed for arable farming. This led to far greater yields, but it also meant that wealthy landowners bought out the small men and deprived cottagers of their rights of pasture on the common, reducing them to landless labourers. Even in the Middle Ages a serf had held some thirty acres of land.

Meanwhile mechanical invention was revolutionizing the cotton and woollen industries. The spinning machine patented by Arkwright in 1769 could do the work of a dozen women, and as it was driven by water power factories were built beside the rapid Pennine streams of Lancashire and Yorkshire. Cartwright invented a power loom

154

Money token, showing a tilt forge, issued by John Wilkinson, 'the great Staffordshire ironmaster'. Iron-mad, he provided by will that he should be buried in an iron coffin.

in 1785, but weaving remained primarily a domestic industry until the machine was perfected some thirty years later, when, like their wives and children before them, weavers became factory employees, divorced from the agents of production which they could no longer afford or work in their homes.

These early machines were made of wood, but they were transformed into iron after Cort's inventions of 1783–4, which by using coal instead of charcoal revolutionized the manufacture of iron. The industry therefore moved from the depleted forest areas to the coalfields on which, now that Watt had discovered how to make the steam engine turn a wheel, the industrial towns of the north sprang up.

James Watt, 1736–1819, whose development of the steam engine led to the Age of Steam: of locomotives, power-driven machinery and factories.

The first railways. By the mid-eighteenth century coal was drawn by horses on light wooden rails.

'The Collier', 1813, the year of 'Puffing Billy', which hauled coal from Wylam Colliery, near Newcastle.

A Staffordshire colliery in the early nineteenth century.

Arthur Young, 1741–1820, Secretary of the Board of Agriculture on its foundation in 1793. He was mainly responsible by his writings for spreading a knowledge of improved farming.

This industrial revolution involved a revolution in transport, and the late eighteenth century saw the making of canals that, in conjunction with the rivers, linked the main ports of England: Hull, Liverpool, Bristol, London. Roads, almost impassable in winter, were also improved, and in 1784 Samuel Palmer was able to start a service of mail coaches.

After 1780, therefore, large-scale production of food and manufactured goods began rapidly to supersede inefficient small-scale farming and the domestic system, dislocating the old way of life much as the decay of manor and guild had dislocated life in Tudor times. The Tudors had dealt with the problem by legislation, but it was now two hundred years out of date, and the eighteenth century believed in *laissez-faire*, non-interference in trade and industry, as expounded by Adam Smith and the new science of Political Economy. Thus, though the wealth of the few was multiplying, the poverty and misery of the many, unprotected by the state, deprived of the means of production, and driven to live in slums and work appallingly long hours for pitifully low wages in factories and mines, young children as well as men and women, were increasing equally rapidly. The country was splitting into two nations of owners and workers, rich and poor.

There was, however, a new spirit abroad. Wesley's preaching had led to an Evangelical movement, whose members believed that religion should be expressed in good works. Among these humanitarians were

The beginning of canal communication in England. The Duke of Bridgewater and the aqueduct that carried his canal across the Irwell on its way from Manchester to his coalfields at Worsley. James Brindley was the engineer. The canal was opened in 1761.

John Howard, the prison reformer, and William Wilberforce, who devoted his life to the abolition of slavery. Perhaps this humanitarianism was not unconnected with the new spirit of liberty in literature; yet, though Johnson was an anti-slavery man, one cannot help wondering what he would have made of the poems of Burns and Blake, published shortly after his death.

Unhappily, the reforming party, the Foxite Whigs, was condemned to half a century of opposition, and the early legislation of Pitt and the new Tory oligarchy was concerned mainly with finance and the colonies. In India the British government assumed control of the administration, leaving the Company to manage commercial affairs. Canada was divided into two provinces: Quebec, whose colonists were mainly French, and Ontario, where most of the Loyalists who had left the United States had settled, each being given a large measure of self-government. In Australia Pitt's policy was less enlightened: the new colony at the far side of the world was to be a convict settlement, and in 1788 the first batch of these unfortunate men and women arrived in Botany Bay.

There were soon to be ample reinforcements. In the following year the French Revolution broke out, and Fox rejoiced, 'How much the greatest event that has happened in the world, and how much the best.' Burke, however, expressed his fears eloquently in *Reflections on the French Revolution*, to which the radical republican Tom Paine replied in his *Rights of Man*: 'Not one glance of compassion . . . has he bestowed on those who lingered out the most wretched of lives . . . He pities the plumage, but forgets the dying bird.' The book had an enormous circulation, but Burke's fears appeared to be justified by the September Massacres of 1792 and execution of the French king. Burke and his followers joined the Tories, thus splitting the Whig party, and the government, thoroughly frightened, embarked on a course of ferocious repression and persecution. The Habeas Corpus Act was suspended, which meant that people could be imprisoned without being brought to trial, a new law of treason was passed, public meetings were banned, cheap newspapers suppressed by the imposition of stamp duties, and the flow of convicts to Australia increased.

Pitt addressing the House of Commons. Fox is in profile on the Opposition bench on the right. The Speaker is Henry Addington, who replaced Pitt as Prime Minister 1801–4. 'Pitt is to Addington as London is to Paddington,' wrote Canning.

There was some reason for alarm, for the exultant revolutionaries promised help to all peoples oppressed by kings, and by the beginning of 1793 the French Republic was at war with Austria, Prussia, Holland, Spain, and in occupation of the Netherlands. War with Britain followed as a matter of course, for it was to prevent the occupation of the Netherlands by a great power that England had fought under Elizabeth and Anne, and was to fight again in the twentieth century.

The position of France seemed hopeless, yet four years later Britain stood alone: Prussia and Austria had surrendered, and Holland and Spain were allies of the French. The year 1797 was one of the most perilous in the history of England. Pitt was no war minister like his father, though he tried to emulate his policy: as Canada had been won in Germany, so the West Indies, then thought to be the most valuable of all possessions, were to be won in Europe. So he paid his allies to fight France in Europe and sent troops to the West Indies, where 40,000 of them perished. Ireland was again on the verge of rebellion, there was danger of French invasion, and mutinies broke out in the fleet. At home, there was a financial crisis, and the food shortage and rise in prices added to the misery of the poor. As wages were so low and the state enforced no minimum, it became the practice of local authorities, following those of Speenhamland, to supplement wages out of rates, recipients being forced to work for a pittance and their children 'apprenticed' to factories. The only action taken by the government was to pass the Combination Acts, which made unions of workers for bettering their lot punishable as unlawful conspiracies.

Despite the mutineers, Britain was saved by her sailors, who defeated the Spaniards at Cape St Vincent, the Dutch at Camperdown, and the French at the Battle of the Nile, Nelson's great victory that forced General Buonaparte to abandon his advance on India and restored British supremacy at sea.

As a result Pitt was able to form a Second Coalition, paying Austria and Russia to fight Napoleon, who in 1799 established himself as First Consul. The coalition did not last long: Napoleon routed the Austrians at Marengo, and Russia formed an Armed Neutrality with Denmark and Sweden against Britain, who once again stood alone. Again she was saved by Nelson, whose destruction of the Danish fleet off Copenhagen broke up the Armed Neutrality, and in 1801 the exhausted protagonists made peace.

It was at this time that Pitt, after the rebellion of 1798, tried to solve the Irish problem by passing an Act of Union, similar to that with Scotland a hundred years before, whereby Ireland returned members to the British Parliament. But these members were Protestants,

Napoleon's projected invasion of England by tunnel, sea and air. A French fantasy.

for though Irish Catholics, unlike those in England, could vote, they could not themselves sit in Parliament, and Pitt's attempt to give them this right was defeated by the obstinacy of the King. The Irish Parliament had been bribed to accept the Union and dissolve itself, and now the country was governed by the Protestant Parliament of the newly formed United Kingdom at Westminster.

For Napoleon the Peace of Amiens was merely a breathing space in which to consolidate his position, and the war with England was renewed in 1803. In 1804 he became Emperor, but his plan to add

The Battle of Trafalgar. Nelson ends Napoleon's plan to invade England, 21 October 1805.

The Battle of Waterloo. Wellington's final defeat of Napoleon, 18 June 1815.

Britain to his European empire was finally shattered by Nelson's crowning victory at Trafalgar. Thwarted at sea, he turned on Pitt's allies of the Third Coalition, and with a series of hammer blows knocked them out one by one, and in 1807 Britain was again alone. In these years death claimed Nelson and Pitt, then Fox, but not before he had carried his motion for the abolition of the slave trade, an even greater and better event, perhaps, than the fall of the Bastille and French despotism.

The war now entered a new phase under new leaders: Castlereagh and Wellington. Napoleon was master of the land, and by his Continental System tried to ruin Britain by excluding her goods from Europe; but Britain was mistress of the sea, and replied by declaring a blockade of all ports from which her trade was excluded, a policy that involved her in an unhappy war with the United States. But the Continental System was Napoleon's undoing, for to enforce his decrees he was compelled to occupy or annex most of the countries of Europe, and thus raised their peoples, far more formidable than governments, against him. His occupation of Spain and Portugal gave Britain her chance of military intervention, and by 1810 Wellington was firmly established behind the lines of Torres Vedras near Lisbon, whence he was able to advance and help the Spanish nationalists. Then in 1812, to bring the Czar to heel, Napoleon occupied Moscow, but only to be fired out by patriots into the Russian winter which destroyed his army. In 1813 the revolted nations defeated him at Leipzig; Wellington routed a French army at Vitoria and crossed the Pyrenees, and in 1814 Napoleon abdicated.

Horatio Nelson, 1758–1805.

Duke of Wellington, 1769–1852.

There followed the epilogue of the Hundred Days, from March to June 1815, when Napoleon escaped from Elba, raised his last army and fought his last battle at Waterloo. The Twenty Years' War was over.

The statesmen who met at Vienna to make the peace showed little appreciation of the popular forces of liberty and nationalism that had been released by the war, and tried to put the clock back to 1789. The eighteenth century was to go on for ever, and there were to be no more revolutions. The old line of French kings was restored, reaction descended on Europe, and Germany, Italy and Poland were carved up without any consideration for their peoples, making further wars and revolutions inevitable.

Thanks to her command of the sea, Britain emerged from the war with a second empire to compensate for the one she had lost forty years before: to Canada, Australia and most of India she had added almost casually in the course of the war Cape Colony, Ceylon and Guiana, all taken from the Dutch, as well as scores of smaller provinces and islands from the West Indies to the East. It was a heterogeneous collection, an immense responsibility and apparently a doubtful asset, for colonies seemed to be more trouble than they were worth, temporary acquisitions soon to go the way of the thirteen American states.

Yet the greatest power in the world was not very far from revolution. Political and economic reform had been overdue before the great war began, but the last twenty years had been a period of repression during which the condition of the poor had steadily deteriorated. Without the right to vote or even to combine to better their condition, they were exploited in factories by the new capitalists and on the land by the old

'The Battle of Peterloo,' 16 August 1819. The end of a demonstration, led by 'Orator' Hunt, against the Corn Laws, in St Peter's Fields, Manchester. A cartoon by T. Tegg.

'A village of unity and mutual co-operation, combining agriculture, manufactures and trade.' Robert Owen's settlement at Orbiston, near Glasgow, 1825. It lasted only two years.

aristocracy, the members and controllers of Parliament, whose first measure after the war was a Corn Law to keep up rents by prohibiting the import of cheap foreign grain. And this at a time when the population was multiplying, for poverty and squalor are great breeders of children. Peace failed to bring plenty, for Europe was too impoverished to buy British manufactures, and the Corn Law was followed by riots, riots by repression, and repression by riots, culminating in the 'Massacre of Peterloo' in Manchester, when eight demonstrators were killed and hundreds injured by a charge of the yeomanry. The government congratulated the magistrates on their action, and passed the Six Acts, amounting almost to a suspension of the constitution and provoking the Cato Street Conspiracy, an attempt to murder the Tory Cabinet.

The people had their champions, however. There was Jeremy Bentham, the crusader for reform of the law and critic of all established institutions, with his utilitarian philosophy of 'the greatest happiness of the greatest number'; Robert Owen, the philanthropic factory owner and father of socialism; William Cobbett, a Tory turned Radical, who looked back nostalgically to the old England of contented village life, thundered against the exploitation of agricultural and factory workers, and taught them that the right to vote was the key to reform. The poets, too, were on their side: Shelley, whose *Prometheus Unbound* appeared in the year of Peterloo, and Byron, soon to lose his life fighting for the liberty of Greece.

The convulsion of the French Revolution and the ensuing war involved a revolution in the arts, and the high hopes and heroism of the period inspired a galaxy of writers comparable to those of the age of Elizabeth, the Armada and twenty years' war with Spain. Breaking with the effete classical tradition of the eighteenth century and discarding its artificial poetic diction, the poets turned for inspiration to nature and wrote in a language more nearly resembling that of everyday life. The first of these revolutionary poems were the *Lyrical Ballads* of Wordsworth and Coleridge, published in 1798, at the time of the Battle of the Nile, and all their best work was done during the war. That of Byron, Shelley and Keats was concentrated within the seven years of Tory reaction after Waterloo, and by 1824 all of them, so young, were dead. Scott's poetry belongs to the last half of the war, and his novels, beginning with *Waverley*, to the peace. Jane Austen, however, was not carried away by the Romantic Movement, romance for her being the unsensational adventures of young lovers in country houses during the war, of which they seem to be quite unaware, and *Northanger Abbey* is a skit on the excesses of the movement, the romantic horrors of the Gothic novel and sham Gothic buildings such as Fonthill Abbey.

Painters were also turning to nature, away from the grandiose classicism and fashionable portraiture of Reynolds and his school. The landscapes of Richard Wilson, a contemporary of Johnson, were unappreciated by the elegant town dwellers of the eighteenth century, but Constable and Turner were more fortunate in their age, and did for painting very much what Coleridge and Wordsworth did for poetry: 'choose incidents from common life', as Wordsworth wrote, 'and throw over them a certain colouring of imagination, whereby ordinary things should be presented to the mind in an unusual aspect'.

These were also great years for British science, when Dalton was expounding his atomic theory, Davy discovering new metals and inventing the miner's safety-lamp, and Faraday beginning his work on electricity, which led to the invention of the dynamo.

The old king died in 1820, blind, insane and unlamented, and was succeeded by the deplorable George IV, who for the last nine years had been Prince Regent. In 1822 Castlereagh committed suicide, the Tory ministry was reorganized to include more liberal members – Canning, Robert Peel and Huskisson – and the post-war period of reaction ended. It was Canning who 'called a New World into existence to redress the balance of the Old', by supporting the independence of Spain's revolted South American colonies, and encouraging President Monroe to pronounce his 'doctrine' that any interference in American affairs by European powers would be opposed by the United States. And it was largely owing to Canning that Greece, long subject to Turkey, regained her independence. At the same time Peel was revising the penal code, Huskisson the tariffs, and in 1824 Pitt's Combination Acts, which had made Trade Unions illegal, were repealed.

A liberal Tory. George Canning, 1770–1827, Foreign Secretary 1822 and Prime Minister 1827.

Trade Union Card, 1833.

169

Wellington and Peel,
Prime Minister and Home
Secretary in 1828.

Even under the ultra-Tory Wellington, who became Prime Minister in 1828 after Canning's death, some reforms were made. Peel, the Home Secretary, created the first efficient police force, the London 'Peelers' or 'Bobbies', and the Test Act, which since 1673 had excluded Catholics and Dissenters from state and municipal office, was abolished. Wellington and Peel, however, were opposed to Catholic emancipation, the right of Catholics to sit in Parliament, but they had either to submit to the demand of Daniel O'Connell, leader of the Irish Catholic Association, or face civil war in Ireland, and in 1829 the Catholic Emancipation Act was passed. This and the other reforms split the Tory party, and at the general election following the accession of William IV in 1830, the Whigs, after sixty years in opposition, were returned with a majority. It was one of the major crises in British history, for the Whigs were pledged to parliamentary reform, while Wellington and his Tory followers were pledged to oppose it by all means in their power.

A Bobby, or Peeler.

That summer the Manchester and Liverpool railway was opened,
Stephenson's 'Rocket' attaining a speed of thirty-five miles an hour,
much to the alarm of the public, who foresaw a world without birds and
horses, milkless cows, eggless hens and a general conflagration. The
railway and radical reform came in together.

George Stephenson
and 'The Rocket'.

The modern railway really begins with the opening of the
Liverpool and Manchester line in 1830. 'A train
of the first-class of carriages, a train of the second-class
for outside passengers', and two goods trains.

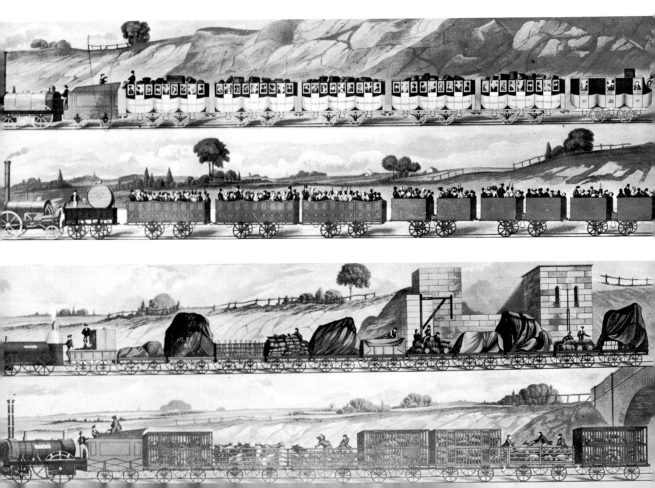

The electoral franchise and distribution of seats in Parliament were the accumulated muddle of centuries. Since 1430 the forty shilling freeholders had elected county members, but there was no standard qualification for the boroughs. Many of them were pocket or rotten boroughs: six peers nominated forty-five members, and sometimes a single voter returned two for the Cornish hamlet of Bossiney. Only one person in a hundred had the vote, and new industrial towns like Manchester and Birmingham were unrepresented in Parliament. This was

The Reformed Parliament, 1833, with the Prime Minister,

the 'system' that the Iron Duke considered incapable of improvement and was prepared to defend to the last.

The year 1830 was one of revolution in Europe, and of great distress in England, of strikes in towns and riots in the countryside. Reform was essential, and Lord Grey's Whig government, which included Lord Durham and Lord John Russell, drew up a Bill that abolished rotten boroughs and gave their seats to new towns, enfranchised ten pound householders in boroughs and fifty pound tenants in the counties.

Lord Grey, and members of his Whig government that carried out sweeping reforms.

The Earl of
Shaftesbury,
1801–85, friend
of the oppressed: of
the lunatic, factory hand,
chimney-sweep,
ragged urchin and
slum-dweller.

It was thrown out by the Lords, but eventually forced through by the King's agreeing to create a majority of Whig peers, and in 1832 it became law.

It was one of the most important events in British history, and may have saved the country from revolution: instead of an order imposed on the people by the king or an aristocracy, the people themselves were to create a new order; or rather, some of the people, for it was only the middle classes, and only men, who had received the vote, but it was the necessary first step towards democracy. The Whig aristocrats still formed the government, but many of the members of the newly elected Commons were plebeian, and out of this alliance of the aristocratic Whigs with the middle classes the democratic Liberal party was to evolve.

The reformed Parliament lost no time, and in 1833 passed a series of revolutionary measures. The slave trade had been abolished in 1807, and now the work of Wilberforce was triumphantly completed in the year of his death by the abolition of slavery, £20,000,000 being voted to compensate slave owners in the colonies. Then, largely owing to Lord Shaftesbury, the first effective Factory Act was passed, limiting the hours worked by children in cotton factories to nine, prohibiting their employment under nine years of age and, very important, appointing inspectors to see that the provisions were enforced. It was a modest beginning, as was the Treasury grant of £20,000 a year to the Church societies who were educating young children, but it was a recognition that the State was responsible for the conditions of employment and education of its citizens. The State also assumed responsibility for the poor, a duty so long neglected since the breakdown of the Tudor Poor Law. As the Speenhamland system of subsidizing wages out of rates had prevented a rise in wages and demoralized the labourers, the Poor Law of 1834 enacted that the able-bodied poor must go to workhouses for relief, where conditions were to be less attractive than those of the worst-paid free labour. Although some such reform was essential, the Act was unimaginatively harsh, and lost the Whig government much of its popularity with the working classes. For the Municipal Reform Act, however, there could be nothing but praise, for it made towns

The Abolition of
Slavery in the British
Empire, 1833.

above a certain size responsible for their own affairs through munici-
palities elected by all ratepayers, an invaluable training in democratic
government. Meanwhile, Grey's ministry had supported the Belgians
of the Netherlands in their revolt against the Dutch, to whom they had
been joined after the war, and it was largely owing to Palmerston, the
Foreign Secretary, that the new kingdom of Belgium was established
and its neutrality guaranteed. Britain had fought three long wars to keep
a great power out of the Netherlands, and for nearly another century
she had nothing to fear from that quarter.

In 1834 Grey resigned to make way for a new Prime Minister,
Lord Melbourne. By this time the reforming zeal of the Whigs had
slackened, and when Victoria came to the throne in 1837 – the year
of *Pickwick Papers* – Melbourne devoted himself to teaching the young
Queen the duties of a constitutional sovereign, lessons that she was
never to forget. Her accession came at an unhappy time, however. The
government, frightened of the incipient Trade Unions, had prosecuted
six labourers who had formed a lodge at Tolpuddle in Dorset and been
transported on a charge of sedition, and the working classes, infuriated
by this injustice and the inhumanity of the Poor Law – *Oliver Twist*,
Dickens's protest against the workhouses, was appearing in serial form
– had lost faith in the Whigs and their middle-class allies, and were
clamouring for far more radical political reform as a means of redressing
their wrongs. A People's Charter was drawn up demanding universal

'Child as he was, he was desperate with hunger, and
reckless with misery. He rose from the table, and
advancing to the Master, basin and spoon in
hand, said, "Please, sir, I want some more."'
Cruikshank's original illustration to *Oliver Twist*, 1837.

Child labour in the coal mines
before the Mines and
Collieries Act of 1842.

Queen Victoria on her accession in 1837, aged eighteen. A painting by Sir George Hayter.

Prince Albert of Saxe-Coburg, 1819–61, who married his cousin Victoria in 1840.

suffrage, and a monster petition presented to Parliament. Its rejection was followed by riots at Newport, the transportation and imprisonment of Chartist leaders, and by 1840 the movement was, for the time being, defeated.

A more enlightened policy was being pursued in the colonies. In 1837 there were rebellions in the two Canadian provinces of Ontario and Quebec, the one with its English settlers, the other mainly French, and it looked as though the colony was going the way of the thirteen American states; but Lord Durham's recommendations were embodied in the Canada Act which united the two, and by 1846 the colony was completely self-governing. This was a new concept of Empire: the colonies were to be bound to the mother country by freedom, and a few years later those in Australia were given internal self-government. Moreover, Gibbon Wakefield persuaded the British government to assist emigration to Australia and New Zealand, which was annexed in 1840. A more liberal policy was also adopted in India, where 'no native, or any natural-born subject of His Majesty, shall be disabled from holding any place, office or employment by reason of his religion, place of birth, descent or colour,' and, for good or ill, English was to become the official language. In South Africa, however, thousands of Boer farmers, angered by inadequate compensation for their slaves and inadequate protection from native tribes, set out from Cape Colony on their Great Trek to settle in the territory north of the Orange and Vaal rivers.

The Hungry Thirties passed into the Hungry Forties; the Queen married her cousin, Prince Albert of Saxe-Coburg, and in 1841 Melbourne's ministry fell, the Poor Law having lost them Radical support, and the Factory Act that of the Liberal manufacturers. The condition of the workers was appalling: agricultural wages were ten shillings a week, as were those in cotton factories, and thousands of city dwellers

The Great Trek of 1836–8 – a bullock waggon crossing a mountain.

Richard Cobden, 1801–65, addressing a meeting of the Council of the Anti-Corn Law League.

had only a shilling a week to live on, the price of a loaf of bread. The Chartist movement was revived, and Cobden and Bright, two cotton manufacturers, founded an Anti-Corn Law League.

Fortunately there was an alternative to the Whigs in the new Conservative party that Peel had created out of the ruins of the old Tory party. Although pledged to retain the Corn Laws, Peel was impressed by the free trade arguments of Cobden and Bright: 'We must make this country a cheap country for living,' he wrote, and in 1842 abolished hundreds of import duties, making up the deficit with an income tax, a temporary measure that was never to be removed. The weakness of the Whigs had been their lack of a great finance minister, but Peel's financial reforms gave the country the stimulus that it needed, and in 1846, when a potato famine threatened Ireland with starvation, he crowned his life's work by abolishing the Corn Laws. It broke the Conservative party, but may have saved England from revolution in the perilous year of 1848, for by that time the country was set fair for prosperity. The new policy of free trade instead of protection meant cheap food and more exports from 'the workshop of the world', for the Industrial Revolution had scarcely begun outside Britain; a Mines Act and another Factory Act improved the shocking working conditions, and the developing network of railways gave employment to thousands of 'inland navigators', or navvies.

The Whigs inherited the benefits of Peel's reforms and, while Disraeli was resurrecting the Conservative party, enjoyed a further twenty years of scarcely interrupted power, the heyday of mid-Victorian prosperity, when social problems were largely forgotten and the main interest was in the foreign policy of Palmerston. When, therefore, in 1848, most of Europe was convulsed in revolution, the worst that Russell's ministry had to face was another Chartist petition and another hopeless rebellion in Ireland. Chartism died a natural death, and political agitation gave place to a constructive trade unionism – the first great national union, the Amalgamated Society of Engineers, was founded in 1851 – but many thousands in Ireland had died of starvation during the famine, and thousands more sailed for America, carrying in their hearts a detestation of England.

'Equal Representation; Universal Suffrage; Vote by Ballot . . .' A Chartist meeting on Kennington Common, 1848.

Nothing of this Irish misery, or of that of the working classes, now championed by Charles Kingsley and other Christian Socialists, was to be seen at the Great Exhibition of 1851, the triumphant expression of British supremacy and middle-class prosperity. The new Poet

The beginning of mid-Victorian prosperity. The Great Exhibition in Hyde Park, Prince Albert's conception, opened by the Queen, 1 May 1851: 'The *happiest, proudest* day in my life. Albert's dearest name is immortalized.'

Laureate, Tennyson, wrote an Ode:

> Lo! the long laborious miles
> Of Palace; lo! the giant aisles,
> Rich in model and design.

Seeing the Old Year out and the New Year in.

The beginning of the Palmerstonian decade, 1855–65.

Whatever we may think today of these Victorian 'shapes and hues of Art divine', Britain could at least congratulate herself on her writers. The poetry of the age was dominated by Tennyson and Browning – *In Memoriam* was published in 1850; Carlyle was writing his *Frederick the Great*, and Macaulay, a member of Russell's Government, his *History of England*; *David Copperfield*, *Vanity Fair*, *Wuthering Heights* and *Jane Eyre* were all new novels in 1851, the year of Ruskin's *Stones of Venice*. For Ruskin the thirteenth century was the great period of European art – the Houses of Parliament, burned down in 1834, were being rebuilt in the late Perpendicular style – and he warmly supported the only revolution in England in 1848, that of the Pre-Raphaelite Brotherhood of Holman Hunt, Millais and Rossetti, with its aim of returning to the simplicity of early Italian painting. Another form of return to Italy was the going-over to Rome of Newman, Manning and other members of the Oxford Movement, which encouraged the Pope once again to appoint Roman Catholic bishops in England, despite the protests of Russell.

The Great Exhibition in Hyde Park was the economic counterpart of the political exhibition at the Foreign office, where Palmerston, flaunting the power of Britain, recklessly displayed his sympathy for the liberal cause in Europe and his detestation of foreign despotism, even being prepared to use the fleet to right the wrongs of a British subject in Athens, a Portuguese Jew who had been born in Gibraltar. His jaunty jingoism led at length to his dismissal, but he soon had his revenge, when he carried an amendment to a Militia Bill which forced Russell to resign.

The Whig party was now split as well as the Conservative, and neither could command a majority without the help of Peel's followers, the Conservative free traders. Peel had just died, but Lord Aberdeen formed a Coalition government with the Whigs, the other leading Peelite being Gladstone at the Exchequer. Palmerston accepted the Home Office.

It was this government that went to war with Russia in 1854, in support of the tottering Turkish empire in the Balkans, which Palmerston saw as a bulwark against Russian expansion. The campaign was fought, in alliance with France, in the Crimea, where the incompetent command that allowed the heroic blunder of the Light Brigade's charge and the loss of the lives of thousands of wounded men swept Palmerston into Aberdeen's place as Prime Minister, where he remained for the next ten years. He brought the war to a victorious conclusion in 1856, but the peace settled nothing, and the real victory was that of Florence Nightingale, who, by her devotion to the wounded and genius for organizing, reduced deaths in the military hospitals to a fraction of what they had been, thus inspiring a new conception of the capacity of women, which ultimately brought about their emancipation.

Florence Nightingale (1820–1910), heroine of the Crimean War, whose character and mission were summed up in the anagram, *Flit on, cheering angel.*

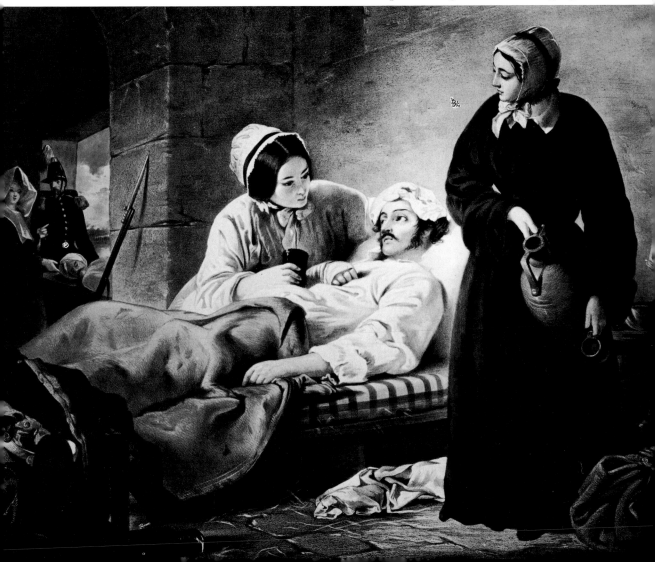

The Crimean War was followed in 1857 by the Indian Mutiny. Dalhousie's annexation of Oudh and his over-rapid introduction of western ways had caused a general unease, which crystallized into mutiny when the sepoys were issued with cartridges greased with the fat of the sacred cow and abominable pig. Fortunately the trouble was confined mainly to one area, the upper Ganges, from Delhi to Cawn-pore and Lucknow, and by the autumn of 1858 it was over. As a result, the East India Company was abolished, the British government assuming complete control, and the policy of annexing protected native states was abandoned.

One foreign crisis followed another, and Palmerston, darling of the people, was in his element. In 1859–60 came Italy's struggle for unity, and it was partly owing to Palmerston, Russell and Gladstone, who encouraged the Italian nationalists and prevented interference by the reactionary powers, that Garibaldi and his Thousand were able to overthrow the foreign despotism in Sicily and Naples and add southern Italy to the north.

The Indian Mutiny – the storming of Delhi and its capture from the mutineers in September 1857.

Lord John Russell, 1792–1878, largely responsible for the first Reform Bill, and Whig Prime Minister 1846–52 and 1865–6.

The American Civil War of 1861–5 was the reverse of this: the attempt of the slave-owning southern states to break away from those of the north. Despite a cotton famine, the British working classes never wavered in their support of Lincoln and the North, but the upper classes favoured the southern gentry, and though the British government behaved correctly on the whole, relations with the victorious North were strained. Partly as a result of this, Ontario, Quebec, New Brunswick and Nova Scotia formed a federation in 1867, so becoming the first self-governing Dominion, the Dominion of Canada.

The last episode in Palmerston's diplomacy ended in humiliation, Bismarck was determined to seize the duchies of Schleswig and Holstein from Denmark, and add them to Prussia. Palmerston blustered, but Bismarck called his bluff and annexed them, with the great harbour of Kiel. Within a year Prussia had routed Austria, and was master of Germany. Perhaps it was just as well that Palmerston died before Bismarck's triumph, for brinkmanship practised against the Iron Chancellor might have ended in something worse than humiliation. Palmerston had had his day, a formidable new European power had appeared, and an era was over.

Like aristocratic Whiggism, Prince Albert too was dead, and his Memorial, in Ruskinian Gothic, rising in Kensington Gardens was also a memorial to the age that had ended. Dickens had written his last novel, and Trollope *The Last Chronicle of Barset*; Matthew Arnold was writing his melancholy poetry and deploring the decay of Culture in an age of upper-class Barbarians and middle-class Philistines; William Morris was protesting against the ugliness of Victorian towns and commercial products, dreaming of Chaucer's London, 'small, and white, and clean', and returning to the craftsmanship of the Middle Ages, while Oxford undergraduates were chanting the revolutionary *Poems and Ballads* of his friend Swinburne. Steamships were replacing sail. England and America were linked by a submarine telegraph cable. In 1859 Darwin published his *Origin of Species*, and John Stuart Mill his essay *On Liberty*; in 1867 came Marx's first volume of *Kapital*, and in the same year the second Reform Bill was passed, giving the vote to another million people, the working classes in towns.

The *Great Eastern*: a very rare photograph of 1862. A barque-rigged iron vessel, driven by screw and paddles, she was used for laying the Atlantic cable 1865-6.

Great and Glorious News for Old England
REFORM BILL PASSED.

SPEED THE PLOUGH.

Peace & Plenty

LORD RUSSELL AND REFORM.
60
Rotten boroughs disfranchised

Rejoicings for the Passing of the Reform Bill.

The Country as it will be.

A Broadsheet celebrating the passing of the 1867 Reform Bill.

The stage was now set for the classic encounter between the new leaders of the two historic parties. Under Gladstone the aristocratic Whig party was transformed into one primarily of middle-class Liberals with a Radical left wing, while in the twenty years since Peel's splitting of the Tories Disraeli had educated country gentlemen into a Conservative party that was prepared to accept instalments of democracy. It was, indeed, Disraeli and the Conservatives who, in an attempt to gain the support of the working class and so 'dish the Whigs', passed the Reform Bill of 1867. The newly enfranchized voters, however, were not grateful, and at the election of 1868 returned the Liberals with a large majority, and Gladstone formed his first and greatest ministry.

Reform, held up during the Palmerstonian era and now inspired by the writings of John Stuart Mill, who modified the extreme *laissez-faire* philosophy of non-intervention by the State, followed in a flood similar to that after the first Reform Act. The Ballot Act made voting secret; the army was reorganized and purchase of commissions abolished;

trade unions were given a legal status, the universities opened to men of all creeds, and in Ireland the Anglican Church was disestablished and a Land Act protected tenants from exploiting landlords. Then, most important of all, the Education Act of 1870 established primary schools where there were no Church schools. Education was neither compulsory nor free, but it was the long overdue beginning of a national system of education, the foundation on which modern society must be built.

These reforms lost the government the support of many vested interests, and when a dispute with the United States was settled in a civilized way by arbitration, damages being awarded against Britain, there was a further decline in popularity in a country accustomed to Palmerstonian bluster. Disraeli, therefore, could taunt Gladstone with betraying British interests and compare his ministry to 'a range of exhausted volcanoes', and at the election of 1874 the Conservatives were

The General election of 1874. Disraeli speaking at the Market Ordinary, Aylesbury (*left*). Gladstone addressing the electors of Greenwich at Blackheath.

returned with a triumphant majority for the first time for thirty years. There were, however, significant additions to this Parliament: two miners whose expenses were paid by their trade union, while fifty-eight Irish members formed an independent party of 'Home Rulers'.

Despite Disraeli's gibe, Gladstone was by no means an exhausted force, though he was an exhausting one, as Queen Victoria had discovered: 'He speaks to me as if I were a public meeting,' she complained. Since the death of the Prince Consort she had withdrawn from her people, and her cloistered widowhood so reduced the popularity of the Crown that a wave of republicanism swept the country, particularly after the establishment of the Third Republic in France in 1870. Gladstone loyally defended his royal mistress, but Disraeli understood her: he flattered, cajoled, drew her again into society and ceremonial, called her 'the Faery', and in 1877 presented her with the title of Empress of India.

For Disraeli, a Jew, was a romantic with visions of oriental grandeur, and his main object was to quicken the interest of the British people in their scarcely regarded empire. He did not neglect home affairs, for, wishing to attach the working class to the Conservative party, he busied himself with slum clearance, public health and the adequate protection of trade unions, but his principal theme was the imperial one. Thus, in 1875 he bought the Suez Canal shares of the improvident Khedive of Egypt. 'Four million sterling!' he wrote to the Queen, 'the entire interest of the Khedive is now yours, Madam.' Which meant that Britain had a controlling interest in the new short route to India. Two years later the government annexed the Boer province of the Transvaal, and when the Eastern Question again became acute, Disraeli, now Earl of Beaconsfield, resumed the Palmerstonian policy of supporting Turkey against Russia. After the Turkish massacre of Bulgarians Gladstone demanded the expulsion of the Turks from Europe 'bag and baggage', but Disraeli sent a fleet to defend them, and music halls echoed to the refrain,

'We don't want to fight; but, by Jingo, if we do,
We've got the ships, we've got the men, we've got the money too.'

Queen Victoria as Empress of India, 1877. The Bill conferring the new title was strongly opposed in Parliament, but the Queen protested that 'it was *her* wish, as people *will* have it, that it has been *forced upon her!*'

Before Britain could intervene, however, the Russians had defeated the Turks, but Disraeli forced a revision of the terms of peace, and a grateful Turkey, left in possession of much of the Balkan peninsula, ceded Cyprus to Britain. Disraeli called it 'Peace with Honour'. Less fortunate adventures in Zululand and Afghanistan ended Disraeli's ministry, and in 1880 Gladstone and the Liberals were again in office.

The flood of reform was resumed: employers were made responsible for accidents to their workpeople, all young children had to go to school, wives could keep their property from their husbands, and in 1884 came the third Reform Act, which gave the vote to agricultural labourers. Reform, however, was hampered by the consequences of Disraeli's foreign adventures: the attempted occupation of Afghanistan was followed by withdrawal; the annexation of the Transvaal by a revolt of the Boers, a British defeat at Majuba, and the granting of internal self-government to the Republic; financial intervention in Egypt by political intervention, the crushing of a nationalist revolt, and disaster in the Sudan, where the fanatical General Gordon was killed at Khartoum by fanatical natives.

Then there was the Irish problem. By their obstructive tactics the Irish Home Rulers were making Parliamentary government almost impossible, and Gladstone tried to conciliate them by another Land Act, and to persuade their leader, Charles Stewart Parnell, to use his influence to prevent the outrages of Fenians and other extremists. His plans were wrecked, however, by the murder of the new Chief Secretary, Lord Frederick Cavendish, in Dublin in 1882. Order had to be preserved by force, but Gladstone had become convinced that the Irish must be given Home Rule, and in 1886 introduced a Bill that would restore the Parliament they had lost by the Union with England in 1801, and give them control of most of their internal, though not external, affairs. Nearly a hundred Liberals rebelled and voted against the Bill. Most of the old-fashioned Whigs and even some of the new Radicals, including Joseph Chamberlain, supported the Conservatives, and at the election the combined forces of Conservatives and Liberal Unionists overwhelmed the Liberal Home Rulers and Irish Nationalists. The Liberal party was broken, and another era was over.

Except for one brief period (1892–95) the Conservatives, who gradually absorbed the Liberal Unionists, were in power for the next twenty years, and for twelve of them the Marquis of Salisbury was Prime Minister.

The Europe, and indeed the world, of 1886 was very different from that of twenty years before, at the end of the Palmerstonian era. For the fifty years 1815–65 Britain had been the undisputed mistress of the world. Secure behind the Channel, her fleets dominated the seas, linking every part of her vast Empire, from Canada to India and Australia. While Europe and the United States had suffered war and revolution, she had remained politically stable and been involved in nothing more serious than a campaign in the Crimea and a mutiny in India. Then, because these upheavals had retarded her competitors at the beginning of the Industrial Revolution, Britain had become literally the workshop of the world from whom all countries were eager to buy, and because of her free trade policy since Peel's reforms of the '40s, her imports of raw materials were cheap, as were her manufactured exports, which her merchant fleet carried to the ends of the earth. And London was the world's financial centre.

In 1886 Britain was still the greatest power, but her position was no longer undisputed. Since the end of the Civil War in 1865 the United States had rapidly progressed, and the wheat of her fertile prairies, carried to the coast by her new railways, flooded free-trade England and precipitated the great agricultural depression of the 1870s and '80s. By 1870 Prussia had forged Germany into a powerful united nation, and Italy, too, was at length united. For the moment wars and revolutions were over, and the nations of Europe and the New World, protecting their infant industries behind high tariff walls, were fast becoming industrial rivals of Britain. They also looked with a jealous eye on her colonial sources of raw materials. The new European powers had no imperial possessions, but a great continent, only recently explored, was ripe for exploitation, and the scramble for tropical and equatorial Africa began with the Belgian penetration of the Congo in 1879. It was a return on a bigger and more dangerous scale to the expansionist nationalism and imperial rivalry of the previous centuries, of England's struggle with Spain, Holland and France. Britain herself was not slow to profit from the partition of Africa, and by the end of the century had added almost another three million square miles to her empire, including Nigeria, Kenya, Uganda, Nyasaland and Rhodesia. The Sudan was reconquered and administered jointly by Britain and Egypt, and only German East Africa (Tanganyika) blocked a route through British or British-controlled territory from Cape Town to Cairo. Symbolic of this expansion of empire were the Jubilees of Queen Victoria in 1887 and 1897, celebrated with imperial pageantry, and the occasion of the first two Colonial Conferences.

Fifty Years a Queen. The Golden Jubilee of June 1887, when Victoria was 'surrounded by the most brilliant, royal and princely escort that had ever accompanied a British sovereign'.

Imperial, foreign and Irish affairs absorbed much of the energy of Salisbury's first ministry, and the most important piece of home legis-lation was the Local Government Act of 1888, which set up elected County Councils to replace the justices of the peace who had ad-ministered county business since Tudor times. Education was made free, a Factory Act and Housing Act were passed, yet many, perhaps most, of the working class still lived in almost unbelievable squalor. This was partly because trade unions were confined to skilled trades, and unorganized, unskilled workers were easy prey for exploiting employers. But successful strikes of match-girls, gas workers and dockers in 1888–9 led to a New Unionism of less skilled trades, more militant than the old conservative unions like the Amalgamated Society of Engineers.

The New Trade Unionism: unskilled workers unite. Demand of the newly formed Gas Workers' Union for an eight-hour day, 1889. This was followed by the formation of the Dockers' Union and the successful strike for a wage of sixpence an hour, 'the dockers' tanner'.

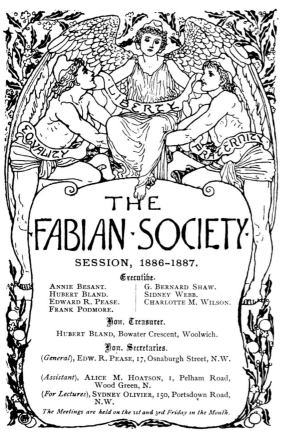

The Fabian Society, founded in 1884, moulded the thought of the Socialist revival. Among its most influential early members were Sidney Webb and Bernard Shaw.

Keir Hardie, 1856–1915, founder of the Independent Labour Party and, with Ramsay Macdonald, of the Labour Party.

Parallel to this development of trade unionism was the revival of socialism, a revolt against nineteenth-century *laissez-faire* and individualism, and an attempt to establish an order based on co-operation and collective ownership. Robert Owen had inspired a number of socialist experiments at the beginning of the century, but it was not until 1844 that the first successful Co-operative Society had been founded. Trade unionism was another aspect of this economic co-operation, and then in the '80s came the political bodies: the Social Democratic Federation and the Fabian Society, the one with a revolutionary Marxist programme, but never a large following, the other composed mainly of middle-class members who believed in evolutionary socialism. Then in 1893 Keir Hardie founded the Independent Labour Party with the object of putting up Labour candidates for Parliament, and in 1900 a conference of Trade Unions, Socialist societies and the Co-operative Movement formed a Labour Representation Committee, or more familiarly, the Labour Party.

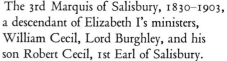

The 3rd Marquis of Salisbury, 1830–1903, a descendant of Elizabeth I's ministers, William Cecil, Lord Burghley, and his son Robert Cecil, 1st Earl of Salisbury.

The last decade of the century was a troubled one. Gladstone's campaign for Home Rule was strengthened when Parnell was proved to be the innocent victim of a forged letter professing to show that he was responsible for the outrages in Ireland, though his subsequent appearance in a divorce case alienated many of his supporters. He died shortly before the election of 1892, when the combined Gladstonian Liberals and Irish Home Rulers gained a small majority. Gladstone introduced a second Home Rule Bill but it was rejected by the Lords and he retired, leaving the premiership to Lord Rosebery. Effective Liberal government was impossible, however, with a Conservative House of Lords in constant opposition, and by 1895 Salisbury was back with a powerful Conservative majority.

By this time the European situation had seriously deteriorated. The international struggle for colonies had degenerated into an international arms race, and the great powers of Europe were split into two rival camps, the Triple Alliance of Germany, Austria and Italy, and the Dual Alliance of France and Russia. Britain stood aloof in 'splendid isolation', though she was almost involved in war in 1898 when the French planted their flag at Fashoda in the Sudan, just reconquered by Kitchener. In the same year Germany began the building of a fleet whose mission was to wrest command of the seas from Britain, and encouraged the Boers in their resistance to British demands.

In 1886 the great gold fields of the Witwatersrand in the Transvaal had been discovered, and the country was invaded by a host of adventurers, most of them British, who quite changed the character of the Boer Republic of conservative farmers, and President Kruger refused to grant them the political rights they demanded. In 1895 Dr Jameson led a disastrous revolt of the 'Uitlanders', in 1899 the British government demanded that they should be given the vote, and the Boers of the Transvaal and Orange Free State declared war. World sympathy was with the Boers, who held out until 1902, when the two states were annexed to the British Crown.

The Relief of Ladysmith in Natal, February 1900, where a British force had been besieged by the Boers. A turning-point in the South African War of 1899–1902.

The wearer of the crown was Edward VII, for Queen Victoria, his mother, had died at the very beginning of the new century, in January 1901. Few of the famous, familiar Victorians survived her; Gladstone, Tennyson, Ruskin had recently gone, and Salisbury retired and died soon afterwards. He was succeeded as Prime Minister by A. J. Balfour, under whom the important Education Act of 1902 was passed, making the new County Councils responsible for both elementary and secondary education. The age of Conservative dominion was almost over, however. In 1903 Joseph Chamberlain, Radical-Unionist-Imperialist, began his campaign for Tariff Reform and Imperial Preference, which meant a return in some measure to the Tory protectionism of the early 1840s, before Peel broke his party by embracing free trade and abolishing the Corn Laws. But in the last half century Britain had grown rich on free trade, its people were not yet convinced of the advantage of change, and Chamberlain split the Conservative party again. Balfour had to resign, and at the election of 1906 the Liberals, as champions of free trade, gained 220 more seats than the Conservatives.

One of the leaflets that helped the Liberals to win a decisive victory at the 1906 election.

The first flight of the first man-carrying aeroplane, at Kitty Hawk, North Carolina, by the American brothers, Orville and Wilbur Wright, 17 December 1903.

A ten-horsepower, two-cylinder Rolls-Royce, 1905.

The last two decades of the nineteenth century had been a period of revolutionary scientific discovery and invention: the invention of new methods of communication in the telephone, wireless telegraphy and cinematograph, of new sources of power in the petrol engine and electricity, of a new mode of transport in the motor car. At the same time Joseph Lister was developing his antiseptic surgery, Huxley vindicating Darwin's theory of evolution and J. J. Thompson probing the structure of the atom. In 1903 the Wright brothers' aeroplane made the first petrol-driven flight of 59 seconds, and in 1905 Einstein published his *Restricted Principles of Relativity*. The new science and technology, as well as the other movements of the period, were inevitably reflected in its literature: Huxley's agnosticism in the novels and poetry of Thomas Hardy, socialism in Morris's *News from Nowhere* and the early plays of Bernard Shaw, Imperialism in the poetry of Kipling, while Oscar Wilde mocked middle-class standards and the young H. G. Wells wrote optimistically about *The First Men in the Moon*.

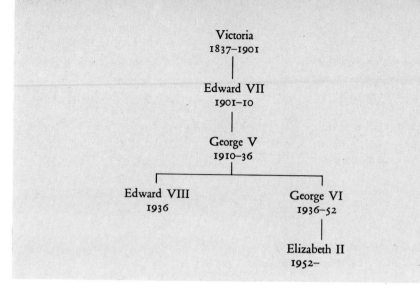

Victoria
1837–1901

Edward VII
1901–10

George V
1910–36

Edward VIII
1936

George VI
1936–52

Elizabeth II
1952–

18
Liberal
Reform
and the
First
World War
1906–1918

Despite the reforms of the nineteenth century there was still little recognition of the duty of society to care for its weaker members. Most men, though no women, now had the vote, and there was an enviable degree of political liberty, of freedom of thought and speech, but the State intervened in the lives of the people as little as possible. Property was protected and the thief severely punished, but there was little protection of the poor against the exploiter, of children, the old, the sick, disabled and unemployed. The time had come for such measures, for prices were rising, real wages – what wages would buy – were falling, and the workers had returned the Liberals to introduce them. They had also returned some fifty Labour members, and these with the Irish Nationalists gave the Liberals a three to one majority over the Conservatives in the Commons. But the Lords, overwhelmingly Conservative, could veto any legislation of which they disapproved.

Under Campbell-Bannerman, and after his death in 1908 under Asquith, the reforms came. School children were to be medically examined and might, when necessary, be given free meals; slums were to be cleared and towns to be planned; the Taff Vale judgment, which had recently made trade unions liable for losses caused by strikes, was reversed; minimum wages were fixed in certain ill-paid industries;

Grave disorder in the House. The Opposition shouting Asquith down as he tries to make his statement on the Bill to curtail the power of the Lords, July 1911.

Labour Exchanges were set up to reduce unemployment, and the condition of old people relieved by a modest pension.

These new functions of the State as protector of its less fortunate members were not only expensive, but involved a new principle: a redistribution of income by taxing the rich to benefit the poor. To find the money, unearned income was taxed more heavily than earned income, though the standard rate was still only 1s 2d, and death duties were increased. Then Lloyd George's Budget of 1909 proposed the levying of a land-tax as well as a super-tax. This was more than the Lords would allow; they had already rejected some of the Bills passed by the Commons, and now they rejected the Budget. By doing so they precipitated the greatest parliamentary crisis since 1832, when they had rejected the Reform Bill, for it was part of Britain's unwritten constitution that the Commons had sole control of finance.

Lloyd George was determined to curb the power of the Lords, but after the general election of January 1910 the two great parties were almost equal, and the Liberals had to rely on the support of Labour and Irish Nationalist members. The position was unchanged by a second election after Edward VII's death in May, and his son George V had to make a momentous decision. The Parliament Bill of 1911 would deprive the Lords of their veto and any control of finance, limiting their power over other Bills to delaying their passage for two years, and reducing the maximum life of a Parliament from seven to five. The Commons passed the Bill and the Lords were invited to sign away their authority. They demurred, but Asquith had persuaded the new king to follow the example of William IV in 1832 and if necessary create a sufficient number of peers to pass the Bill. The Lords surrendered, and the Commons, representing the great mass of the people, became virtually the sole legislative body.

Further reform followed. In 1911 the old Chartist demand of payment of members was carried, and with a salary of £400 working-class men could now afford to sit in Parliament. Two years later the Osborne judgment was reversed, and it became legal for trade unions to use their funds to support Parliamentary candidates. Meanwhile a National Insurance Bill was passed, to give relief to the sick and unemployed out of funds contributed by workers, employers and the State.

Lloyd George discussing the National Insurance Bill with a deputation, December 1911.

Sylvia Pankhurst, leader of the
Suffragettes who demanded votes for
women, addressing a crowd outside
their premises, 1912.

Yet in spite of all these reforms the years were full of bitterness,
industrial unrest and strife. There were serious strikes, particularly of
the miners and railwaymen; the Suffragettes were resorting to violence
to draw attention to their demand of votes for women; Nonconformists
were demanding the disestablishment of the Church in Wales, and
now that the Lords had lost their veto the time had come to satisfy the
Irish Nationalists with a third Home Rule Bill. The Lords, however,
could delay, and the Protestant Ulstermen, who had no wish to be
swamped in a semi-independent Catholic Ireland, used the interval to
import rifles and organize resistance. By 1914 the southern Catholics,
among whom the extremist Sinn Feiners were rapidly gaining ground,
were on the verge of war with the Orangemen of Ulster.

Europe as a whole was in an even more disturbed condition than
Britain, and the breakdown of the old order was prefigured in the
thought and art of the period. In 1909 the Italian *Futurist Manifesto* was

Sir Edward Grey, Liberal Foreign Secretary 1905–16, who tried to prevent the outbreak of war. Behind him (*left to right*) are Winston Churchill, Lloyd George and H. H. Asquith.

published, with its glorification of the machine, violence and war; in 1910 the first Post-Impressionist Exhibition introduced London to the work of the new school of French painters, and *The Times* announced that 'this art is the rejection of all that civilization has done'; in 1913 the new music of Stravinsky's *Rite of Spring* was greeted with catcalls and whistles; Wyndham Lewis and the Vorticists published *Blast*; Le Corbusier was mocking an otiose romanticism and creating a new functional architecture; and in 1914 James Joyce, inspired by Freud's disturbing revelations about man's unconscious mind, began *Ulysses*.

By this time Britain was on the verge of a conflict far greater than the civil war that threatened Ireland. The powers had grabbed their empires, occupying those parts of the world where the people were helpless against western weapons of war, but Germany at least was unsatisfied. Twice she almost went to war with France over Morocco, and when in 1908 her Austrian ally annexed the Serb-inhabited provinces of Bosnia and Herzegovina war threatened with Russia, her rival for influence in the Balkans. Britain drew closer to France and Russia, and as Europe staggered from crisis to crisis the pace of the arms race quickened. Then in June 1914 a Serb murdered the heir to the Austrian Empire. In spite of the peace efforts of Sir Edward Grey, the British Foreign Secretary, Austria declared war on Serbia, Germany on Russia and France, and on 4 August, when German troops had invaded Belgium, Britain declared war on Germany. It was to prevent the occupation of this territory by a great power that England had fought the Spain of Philip II, and the France of Louis XIV and Napoleon. At least it was consolatory that Britain was not alone, but supported by Canada, Australia, New Zealand and South Africa, all of them now independent Dominions. Even India, where nationalist feeling was rising, and Ireland, where Home Rule was postponed, joined in the struggle.

There followed four years of carnage during which the youth of the western world destroyed itself. More nations were drawn into the maelstrom: Turkey on the German side, Italy and Rumania on that of the Allies. Then in 1917 the whole course of the war, and of world history, was changed by the Russian revolution, and the entry of the United States into the European conflict. The end came on 11 November 1918, when the Germans signed an armistice. Britain alone had lost a million men.

'The Menin Road.' Menin is ten miles east of Ypres, a key point held by the British, and scene of some of the most desperate fighting of the First World War.

The signing of the Peace in the Hall of Mirrors at Versailles, 28 June 1919. Wilson, Clemenceau and Lloyd George watch the German delegate sign.

19

*Between
Two Wars
1918–1939*

The young men had fought the war and died, the old men survived and made the peace. It was a vindictive, a Carthaginian peace: Germany lost part of her European territory and all her colonial empire; her fleet was scuttled, her merchant navy divided among the victors, her army reduced to a police force; and finally she was bankrupted by the imposition of reparations that she could never pay. No more effective way could have been devised to ensure a resurgence of German nationalism.

However, thanks to the idealism of President Wilson of the United States, one great creative design emerged from the war to balance the loss and destruction: a League of Nations. Here was something new in international affairs, an institution that would foster co-operation among the nations and check the old unbridled competition that had led inevitably to war, an attempt to apply on the international scale the relationship that man was learning to cultivate with his fellow men. There was to be a General Assembly, a Council, a Court of International Justice, an International Labour Office, and the victors were pledged to reduce their armaments and to administer on behalf of the League the colonies of the vanquished in the interests of the native people. Much was achieved in the following years, though not in the way of disarmament, and the League was crippled from the start by the absence of Russia and the United States which, repudiating Wilson's idealism, withdrew again into transatlantic isolation.

The League of Nations conference in full session at Geneva.

The war had been directed by a Coalition government, first under Asquith, then under Lloyd George, who in 1916 supplanted his old leader, an action that so divided the Liberals that they have never since been in office. In the spring of 1918 the franchise was greatly extended by giving votes to women in recognition of their invaluable war work, and in December the new electorate returned nearly 500 supporters of the Coalition. It was a strange situation: there were twice as many Conservatives as Liberals, yet the Liberal leader, Lloyd George, remained Prime Minister. Asquith's Independent Liberals were reduced to twenty-six, less than half the number of Labour members, who, however, having adopted a new Socialist constitution, refused to support the Coalition, as did the seventy-three Sinn Feiners, pledged not to take their seats at Westminster.

Peace brought two years of booming trade, but the pre-war problems remained, notably Ireland, which had been promised Home Rule. But the attitude of the Sinn Feiners had hardened; there had been a rebellion in Dublin in 1916, and now they demanded an independent republic. A ferocious civil war broke out, and the government tried to crush Irish nationalism by employing ex-soldiers, the Black and Tans, to terrorize the country. Repression failed, Lloyd George had to yield, and at the end of 1921 arrived at a compromise whereby southern Ireland became the Irish Free State, with Dominion status, owing allegiance to the Crown. The extremists, led by de Valera, refused to accept the arrangement, but by 1923 the worst troubles were over. If only a similar settlement could have been made in Tudor times, four centuries of bloodshed and misery might have been avoided, and Ireland might well have become a willing member of the United Kingdom.

In 1920 the feverish post-war boom had sunk into slump, for the world's economy had been disrupted, and the defeated powers were too impoverished to buy. Unemployment rose, and the period was one of depression, hunger marches and strikes, of the writing of *The Waste Land* and *The Hollow Men*, in which T. S. Eliot expressed the disillusion of the early 1920s. They were also years of political instability, owing to the emergence of Labour as a third great party. In 1922 the Con-

The first Labour Government. Ramsay MacDonald in the House of Commons, 1924.

servatives withdrew their support of Lloyd George and the Coalition, and at the election gained a majority over the other two parties. Bonar Law formed a Conservative ministry, but resigned in favour of Stanley Baldwin, who, prescribing protection as a remedy for economic ills, appealed to the country. The combined Labour and Liberal members now outnumbered the Conservatives, and in February 1924 Baldwin was forced to resign, and Ramsay MacDonald, as leader of the next biggest party, formed the first Labour government. It did not last long, and by the end of the year Baldwin was again in office with a huge majority. Labour had 150 seats, but the Liberals were reduced to 40. In future the struggle was going to be one primarily between Conservative and Labour.

The General Strike, May 1926. Armoured cars escort a food convoy in the East India Dock. The strike lasted only ten days.

Baldwin's Chancellor of the Exchequer, Winston Churchill, imposed a number of import duties to protect home industries, but his return to the gold standard, by raising the external value of the pound, made British goods more expensive for foreign countries to buy, and the depression deepened. Conditions were particularly bad in the coal fields, where the owners were demanding longer hours and lower wages, though the General Council of the Trades Union Congress promised to support the miners in their resistance. Baldwin spoke to the nation by the new medium of the wireless, but on 3 May 1926 a General Strike began. Ten days later the Council surrendered, but it was November before the miners were defeated, their plight much worse than before. So was that of trade unionism as a whole, which was further weakened by Acts that reduced its powers. This unsympathetic treatment cost the Conservatives their supremacy. At the election of

'Some 2000 hunger marchers have arrived in London from all parts of Britain.' The unemployed commandeering lorries to evade the police, October 1932.

1929 Labour, supported by the Liberals, had a slight majority, and MacDonald formed his second ministry.

It was an unfortunate time to take office. In September came the great American slump, and by 1931 Europe was on the verge of financial collapse. Britain was driven off the gold standard, there were three million unemployed, and to meet the crisis MacDonald formed a Coalition, or 'National Government', and appealed to the country. The Labour party was broken; only 52 members were returned to oppose the phalanx of 471 Conservatives and their 'National Liberal' and 'National Labour' allies, led by MacDonald, now virtually a Conservative Prime Minister.

So began one of the most disastrous and inglorious decades in our history, and the prelude to a second World War. While the unemployed, their 'dole' now subject to a means test, resumed their hunger marches,

Neville Chamberlain returns with the Munich Agreement after his visit to Hitler, 30 September 1938.

And negotiation wins,
*   If you can call it winning,*
And here we are – just as before – safe in our skins;
*   Glory to God for Munich.*
And stocks go up and wrecks
*   Are salved and politicians' reputations*
Go up like Jack-on-the Beanstalk; only the Czechs
*   Go down and without fighting.*

(Louis MacNeice)

Japan invaded Manchuria. The League of Nations protested, but took no action, and Japan resigned from the League, as did Germany after Hitler's rise to power in 1933. In 1935 Baldwin succeeded MacDonald as leader of the National Government, and acquiesced in Italy's invasion of Abyssinia. In 1936 Hitler occupied the Rhineland, and the Spanish Civil War broke out. Even in England there were clashes between Communists and Oswald Mosley's Fascists, and the poets of the period – Auden, Day Lewis, Spender, MacNeice – passionately protested against the drift to disaster.

At home, the death of George V was followed by the unhappy episode of Edward VIII's abdication, and in 1937 Neville Chamberlain succeeded Baldwin. Acquiescence in aggression was to become appeasement. Japan launched a full-scale war against China, and Italy left the League of Nations, now reduced to impotence. In 1938

Hitler incorporated Austria in Germany, and in September demanded part of Czechoslovakia. Chamberlain went to Munich and returned with what he called, in Disraeli's phrase, 'Peace with Honour', the price being a defenceless Czechoslovakia. In the spring of 1939 Mussolini occupied Albania, and Hitler seized Czechoslovakia. Poland would be next, and at last Chamberlain made a stand by 'guaranteeing', as France had already done, Polish territory against aggression. British industry was recovering, and unemployment fell to little more than a million, for the country was rearming. A few months later Hitler demanded Danzig and the Polish Corridor, which since the last war had separated East Prussia from the rest of Germany. In August he made a non-agression pact with Stalin; on 1 September his troops invaded Poland, and on the 3rd Britain and France were at war with Germany.

The Battle of Britain August 1940. The equivalent, in another element, of the battles of the Armada, La Hogue and Trafalgar.

Britain was fortunate indeed in finding a war leader of the same indomitable quality as Chatham. In May 1940 Churchill replaced Chamberlain, a few weeks before the British troops were driven out of France, and France surrendered. Italy joined Germany, and for a year, the most critical in our history, Britain stood alone. Attempted

D Day, 6 June 1944. During the night, while heavy bombers attacked German defences on the Normandy coast, and five British and American airborne divisions landed behind their lines, an armada of some 4000 ships and several thousand smaller craft sailed down the Channel from the Isle of Wight. By dawn they were off the coast of Normandy, and, supported by bombers and a naval bombardment, the allied landing began. There was little immediate resistance. The Germans had been taken by surprise. It was the beginning of the end.

VE Day. On 7 May 1945 Germany surrendered unconditionally, and hostilities in Europe ceased at midnight on 8 May, though the war with Japan was not over. Mr Churchill spoke to the nation: 'We must make sure that those causes which we fought for find recognition at the peace table in facts as well as words, and above all we must labour to ensure that the World Organization that the United Nations are creating at San Francisco does not become an idle name.'

invasion was defeated, however, and 'the end of the beginning' came in 1941, when Hitler invaded Russia, and the Japanese attack on Pearl Harbour brought the United States into the war. Final victory was assured after the Russian and British triumphs at Stalingrad and Alamein in 1942: Italy capitulated in 1943, France was liberated in 1944, and in May 1945 Germany surrendered. On 6 August the Americans dropped an atom bomb on Hiroshima, and Japan surrendered. The six-year war was over, and another age had begun.

It was not Churchill, however, who with Stalin and President Truman signed the Potsdam Agreement, whereby Germany was divided into four zones occupied by the victorious powers, but Clement Attlee. At the general election in July the Labour party had gained a two to one majority over the Conservatives. There was no question of ingratitude to Churchill, but the electorate had not forgotten the grim decade of the '30s, and there was to be no return to that. Attlee, therefore, became the first Labour Prime Minister with a majority in the Commons, and the work of reconstruction began.

The new Prime Minister, Mr Attlee, waving to the crowd after the Labour Party's victory at the General Election, 27 June 1945.

A playing place for children, with new houses in the background. The new town of
Crawley, Sussex.

Most of the hospitals, the Bank of England, railways, road-haulage,
civil aviation, gas, electricity and the basic industries of coal and steel
were nationalized. An attempt was made, in spite of shortages, to
implement the Education Act of 1944, which, by raising the school-
leaving age to fifteen, and providing grammar, technical and modern
schools, and grants for university students, went some way towards
equality of opportunity for all. Then, a series of Acts provided insurance
for every major form of need, special care for children and old people,

Elliot School, Putney, built by the London County Council in 1956. One of the first Comprehensive Schools in the country, it is also co-educational.

and a free health service for everybody. Only those who have lived through the between-war years can appreciate the social revolution brought about by this legislation.

Britain, however, was impoverished and exhausted, and the period of the Labour government was inevitably one of austerity, when rationing was even more stringent than during the war. There was a financial crisis in 1947 and another in 1949, when the value of the pound was reduced from four dollars to less than three. This discouraged imports and encouraged exports, and a trade revival began.

The Cold War had already begun. Russia had discovered the secret of the atom bomb, the Chinese Communists were establishing the People's Republic, and the world was divided into a capitalist west and communist east. The Russian attempt in 1948–9 to drive the western powers out of Berlin by blockading the land routes through East Germany was foiled by an air lift, and the United States, Canada, Britain and most of the western powers signed the North Atlantic Treaty, which stated that an attack on one was an attack on all. Russian pressure then turned east, to Korea, which, after the expulsion of the Japanese, had been divided into a communist north and southern republic supported by the United States. When, however, the North invaded the South in 1950, there was no return to the acquiescence in aggression of the '30s; the United Nations, which had succeeded the League of Nations, at once demanded the withdrawal of the North Korean forces. When this was refused, sixteen nations, including the United States and Britain, went to the help of the South, and in 1953 peace was restored, though the country remained divided as before. A South-East Asia Treaty Organization was set up, similar to NATO, Britain again being one of the signatories, a partner in the attempted containment of the communist states. It was clear that supranational collaboration was as important as it had ever been.

George VI had died in 1952, to be succeeded by Elizabeth II, and Churchill was again Prime Minister, for at the 1951 election, when the Liberals were reduced to six, the Conservatives gained a small majority. They accepted the social revolution, the Welfare State and most of the actions of the Labour Government, though they returned road haulage and steel temporarily to private enterprise. In 1955 they increased their majority to fifty-nine, and Churchill resigned in favour of Anthony Eden. There followed a strange reversion to Palmerstonian foreign policy. In 1956 Egypt assumed control of the Suez Canal and, in defiance of the United Nations, Britain and France attacked the new republic. Half of Britain and most of the world protested, Eden resigned, and in January 1957 Harold Macmillan became Prime Minister.

Macmillan's period of office, together with the twelve months of his successor, Lord Home, completed thirteen years of continuous Conservative government. The election of 1964, in which Harold Wilson came to power with a slender majority, was to herald a similarly long period of Labour dominance, punctuated only by the Conservative administration of Edward Heath, whose most notable achievement – which provoked widespread controversy – was to take Britain into the European Economic Community, of which she became a member formally in January 1973. The Heath Government was brought down in 1974 in an election that followed a long-lasting miners' strike – a symptom of Britain's continuing failure to combat the difficulties, and take advantage of the opportunities, of economic life in the post-war world. These economic troubles formed a consistent theme through the history of the 1960s and 1970s and it seemed an appropriately English attempt to solve them when the country's first woman Prime Minister, Margaret Thatcher, was elected as the nation prepared to enter the 1980s.

It was not only economic questions that led England to face, sometimes unwillingly, a new way of life after 1945. The exhaustion of the chief colonial powers after the war, and the ease with which the Japanese had overrun their possessions in south-east Asia, quickened the spirit of nationalism in the subject peoples and encouraged them to revolt. Under Attlee's Labour Government Britain withdrew from India, Burma and Ceylon, and recognized southern Ireland as the independent republic of Eire. The Conservatives pursued a similar policy of withdrawal, and nearly all of Britain's former possessions quickly achieved independence. Many of these new nations became members of the Commonwealth of Nations, a free association of sovereign independent states stretching across the Continents of the world. To be at the centre of this community, offering occasional guidance or employing diplomatic persuasion, was by

Mrs Thatcher wins her third General Election victory, June 1987.

The wedding of the Prince of Wales to Lady Diana Spencer, July 1981.

no means an ignoble role, but without political and military power, and the economic strength to support them, Britain suffered a series of frustrations in her relations with her former colonies.

Two hundred years ago Britain achieved her first empire, when virtually the whole of North America came under her control. It did not last long, but a hundred years later she had a second and even greater empire, and by the 1880s had been for more than half a century the leading power of the world. All that has changed in our own time, and today, dwarfed by other powers, Britain has long lost her supremacy. As the end of the century approaches, however, there are signs that she is finding a different role on the world stage. Despite the conflict over the South Atlantic Falkland Islands, in which British forces defeated an occupying army from Argentina in 1982, this is no longer based on political rule or military power; the one remaining colony of any importance – Hong Kong – is in any case to be returned to Chinese hegemony in 1997. Instead, in the era of Mrs Thatcher, it followed from two new factors, one temporary (the sheer force of personality of the Prime Minister and her close relationship with successive American Presidents), and one of ever-increasing significance (the role of Britain, despite continuing national differences, in a Europe slowly moving towards greater economic and political co-operation). Not everyone welcomed this Europeanization, but an important symbol of it was the Channel Tunnel, which literally united England and Continental Europe when it opened for two-way traffic in the mid-1990s.

Mrs Thatcher's Conservative government, which remained in power throughout the 1980s after further election victories in 1983 and 1987, engaged in a number of measures with far-reaching consequences in the life of the nation – among them the return of gas, steel, telecommunications and other publicly controlled bodies to private ownership; the attempt to inject private enterprise principles into those – such as the National Health Service – that remained; and the sale of council houses and encouragement of home ownership. These changes coincided with others, still connected to political policies, but also a reflection of the volatility and mutability of late twentieth-century life: the rise and fall of inflation, of unemployment and of the stock market, or the temporary economic salvation provided by North Sea oil and gas.

An old institution in new guise: Richard Rogers's Lloyd's Building, opened in 1986. In the next decade, when Lloyd's faced financial difficulties, some people used its physical presence to suggest that the economic gains of the 1980s were show rather than substance.

For some, such as the disaffected former Conservative minister Francis Pym, the country was faced by 'the choice between being divided but rich and being united but poor'. Despite many attempts at realignment between the old Liberals and new centre parties, which made little headway, the nation had become in some respects polarized. There was a distinct air of Mrs Gaskell's *North and South* – a Victorian novel, but very far from Mrs Thatcher's stated wish to revive the spirit of Victorian values – about the geographical distribution of the 1987 Election results: Labour won only 26 of 260 seats south of a line between the Severn and the Wash, while the

Conservatives could find little support in such northern cities as Manchester and Newcastle. The gap between rich and poor; inner city decay and riots in Brixton and Bristol; football hooliganism and an increase in violent crime; what some called the 'crumbling' Health Service and 'deteriorating' state schools – all these confronted any complacency that went with the extreme affluence of other parts of society.

By contrast, England's second Elizabeth, long divorced from the real control of political events, became momentarily a unifying point for many of the country's most positive and widely held feelings. In one sense this merely reflected a growing sense that the English heritage, of which the monarchy was a central feature, had itself become a commodity that could be marketed. At its best, however, it represented a simple delight in the continuing pageantry that accompanied, for example, the wedding of Charles, Prince of Wales, to Lady Diana Spencer in July 1981. Subsequently, as the marriage dream turned into a marriage nightmare and the undistinguished conduct of other members of the family was seized upon by the popular press, the volatility of public sentiment at *fin de siècle* became apparent.

This was to be an uncertain era symbolized first by Margaret Thatcher's successor from November 1990, John Major, whose leadership was challenged by members of his own party, but also by a wide variety of different factors: a rapid fall in respect for those in public life and for traditional institutions; anxieties about long-term job security and government finances for an ageing population; the apparent abandonment of many articles of faith by a revived Labour Party under Tony Blair; and a vociferously expressed concern that English identity was being threatened by submergence in Europe.

The most positive visible force, it seemed, was a growing concern – shared internationally, and embracing all sections of the community – for the environment that had presided over the long history from Stonehenge to the microchip. While this concern still faltered in practice, after two centuries of transformation that began with the Industrial Revolution, it seemed that at last everyone could find common cause in the need to preserve 'England's green and pleasant land'.

Suggestions for Further Reading

One of the finest one-volume histories, from prehistoric times to 1918, is G. M. Trevelyan's *History of England* (1926). A companion volume, beginning in the fourteenth century, is G. M. Trevelyan's *English Social History*. Illustrated editions of both these books (1979 and 1978, respectively) are available. For more detailed study, there are the 14 volumes of *The Oxford History of England* and useful multi-volume histories under the editorships of Robert Blake (Paladin, 1974–) and W. N. Medlicott (Longmans, 1958–). Robert Blake has also edited *The English World: History, Character and People* (1982). The 9 volumes of *The Pelican History of England* describe the development of English society from Roman times to the twentieth century.

Asa Briggs covers the *Social History of Britain* (1983) and *The Pelican Social History of Britain* is in progress. *The Pelican Economic History of Britain* ranges from medieval times to the present day in 3 volumes by M. M. Postan, Christopher Hill and E. J. Hobsbawm. In the same format as this book, there are Concise Histories of *The British Army* by Jock Haswell (1975) and *The British Navy* by Oliver Warner (1975), and also *A Concise History of the British Empire* by Gerald Graham (1970).

For short guides to English art and architecture, see William Gaunt's *Concise History of English Painting* (1964) and David Watkin's *English Architecture: A Concise History* (1979). The volumes of *The Oxford History of English Art* give more extensive attention to particular periods. *The Pelican Guide to English Literature* ranges from Chaucer to the present day, in 7 volumes, and the English literature of the last 200 years, as an expression of various reactions to the industrial revolution, is examined by Raymond Williams in *Culture and Society: 1780–1950* (1961).

Chris Cook has edited a number of useful reference books, including *English Historical Facts, 1603–88* (with J. Wroughton, 1980) and *The Longman Handbook of Modern British History, 1714–1980* (with J. Stevenson, 1983).

PREHISTORIC ENGLAND

Richard Bradley, *The Social Foundations of Prehistoric Britain* (1984).

C. Chippindale, *Stonehenge Complete* (1983).

Timothy Darrill, *Prehistoric Britain* (1987).

ROMAN ENGLAND

Ian Richmond, *Roman Britain* (Pelican, 1955).

H. H. Scullard, *Roman Britain: Outpost of the Empire* (1979).

Peter Salway, *Roman Britain* (Oxford History, 1981).

ANGLO-SAXON ENGLAND

H. P. Finberg, *The Formation of England 500–1042* (1974).

H. R. Loyn, *Anglo-Saxon England and the Norman Conquest* (1962).

R. I. Page, *Life in Anglo-Saxon England* (1970).

Sir Frank Stenton, *Anglo-Saxon England* (Oxford History, 3rd ed., 1971).

Dorothy Whitelock, *The Beginnings of English Society* (Pelican, 1952).

D. M. Wilson, *The Anglo-Saxons* (2nd ed., 1971).

THE EARLY MIDDLE AGES

Sir Arthur Bryant, *Makers of the Realm* (1953).

D. C. Douglas, *William the Conqueror* (1964).

Elizabeth M. Hallam, *Domesday Book Through Nine Centuries* (1986).

A. L. Poole, *From Domesday Book to Magna Carta* (Oxford History, 2nd ed., 1955).

Sir Maurice Powicke, *Stephen Langton* (1965).

— *The Thirteenth Century* (Oxford History, 2nd ed., 1962).

Shakespeare, *King John*.

Doris Mary Stenton, *English Society in the Early Middle Ages (1066–1307)* (Pelican, 1965).

W. Warren, *Henry II* (1973).

THE LATER MIDDLE AGES

Sir Arthur Bryant, *The Age of Chivalry* (1963).

Chaucer, *The Canterbury Tales*, for an incomparable picture of late fourteenth-century England. They should be read in the original, but as an introduction there is a modernized version (Penguin) by Nevill Coghill.

E. F. Jacob, *The Fifteenth Century* (Oxford History, 1961).

M. H. Keen, *England in the Later Middle Ages* (1972).

May McKisack, *The Fourteenth Century* (Oxford History, 1959).

A. R. Myers, *England in the Late Middle Ages* (Pelican, 1952).

The Paston Letters illuminate the fifteenth century.

Charles Ross, *The Wars of the Roses: A Concise History* (1976).

Shakespeare's History Plays, from *Richard II* to *Henry VIII*, are a splendid panorama of the fifteenth century.

THE TUDORS

S. T. Bindoff, *Tudor England* (Pelican, 1950).

J. B. Black, *The Reign of Elizabeth* (Oxford History, 2nd ed., 1959).

A. G. Dickens, *The English Reformation* (1964).

G. R. Elton, *England under the Tudors* (2nd ed., 1974).

David Loades, *The Tudor Court* (1986).

J. D. Mackie, *The Earlier Tudors* (Oxford History, 1952).

J. E. Neale, *Queen Elizabeth* (1934).

A. F. Pollard, *Wolsey* (1929).

A. L. Rowse, *The Elizabethan Renaissance*, 2 vols (1972).

— *The England of Elizabeth* (1950).

— *The Expansion of Elizabethan England* (1955).

J. J. Scarisbrick, *Henry VIII* (1968).

Penry Williams, *The Tudor Regime* (1979).

THE STUARTS

Maurice Ashley, *England in the Seventeenth Century* (Pelican, 1952).

— *The English Civil War: A Concise History* (1975).

G. E. Aylmer, *Rebellion or Revolution? England 1640–1660* (1986).

Sir Winston Churchill, *Marlborough*, 2 vols (1947).

Sir George Clark, *The Later Stuarts* (Oxford History, 2nd ed., 1956).

Godfrey Davies, *The Early Stuarts* (Oxford History, 2nd ed., 1959).

Christopher Hill, *Change and Continuity in 17th Century England* (1973).

Ronald Hutton, *The Restoration* (1985).

J. P. Kenyon, *Stuart England* (1986).

Samuel Pepys, *The Diary*, covers the years 1660–9.

I. Roots, *The Great Rebellion, 1642–1660* (1966).

H. R. Trevor-Roper, *Archbishop Laud* (1940).

C. V. Wedgwood, *The King's Peace* (1955).

— *The King's War* (1958).

— *Thomas Wentworth, 1st Earl of Strafford* (1961).

Basil Willey, *The Seventeenth Century Background* (1962).

THE EIGHTEENTH CENTURY

Jeremy Black (ed.), *Britain in the Age of Walpole* (1985).

James Boswell, *The Life of Johnson*.

R. Hatton, *George I, Elector and King* (1979).

D. Jarrett, *England in the Age of Hogarth* (1986).

J. H. Plumb, *England in the Eighteenth Century* (Pelican, 1950).

— *The Growth of Political Stability in England 1675–1725* (1967).

— *Sir Robert Walpole*, 2 vols (1956 and 1960).

A. F. Scott, *The Early Hanoverian Age 1714–1760* (1980).

J. S. Watson, *The Reign of George III* (Oxford History, 1960).

R. J. White, *The Age of George III* (1968).

Basil Willey, *The Eighteenth Century Background* (1962).

A. F. B. Williams, *The Whig Supremacy* (Oxford History, 1960).

THE NINETEENTH CENTURY

Robert Blake, *Disraeli* (1966).

Asa Briggs, *Iron Bridge to Crystal Palace: Impact and Images of the Industrial Revolution* (1979).

G. Kitson Clark, *An Expanding Society, Britain 1830–1900* (1967).

John W. Derry, *William Pitt* (1962).

Sir Robert Ensor, *England 1870–1914* (Oxford History, 1936).

Elizabeth Longford, *Victoria R.I.* (1964).

P. Mathias, *The First Industrial Nation* (1969).

David Thomson, *England in the Nineteenth Century* (Pelican, 1964).

Sir L. Woodward, *The Age of Reform* (Oxford History, 2nd ed., 1962).

THE TWENTIETH CENTURY

Peter Calvocoressi, *The British Experience 1945–1975* (1978).

D. Childs, *Britain Since 1945: A Political History* (1984).

R. S. Churchill and M. Gilbert, *Winston S. Churchill, a Biography* (1966–).

Sir Winston Churchill, *The Second World War*, 6 vols (1948–54).

Sir Philip Magnus, *King Edward the Seventh* (1964).

Arthur Marwick, *The Home Front: The British and the Second World War* (1978).

— *Britain in Our Century* (1984).

Donald Read, *Edwardian England* (1972).

K. Robbins, *The Eclipse of a Great Power: Modern Britain 1870–1975* (1983).

Anthony Sampson, *The Changing Anatomy of Britain* (1983).

A. J. P. Taylor, *English History, 1914–1945* (Oxford History, 1965).

David Thomson, *England in the Twentieth Century* (Pelican, 1965).

List of Illustrations

Index